AMERICAN
WAR LIBRARY

★ The Cold War ★

THE COLD WAR ENDS:
1980 TO THE
PRESENT

by Britta Bjornlund

LUCENT
BOOKS®

THOMSON

GALE

San Diego • Detroit • New York • San Francisco • Cleveland • New Haven, Conn. • Waterville, Maine • London • Munich

On cover: President Ronald Reagan and Soviet leader Mikhail Gorbachev (right) leave the podium after a 1987 White House ceremony welcoming Gorbachev. A Russian interpreter follows behind the two leaders.

© 2003 by Lucent Books. Lucent Books is an imprint of The Gale Group, Inc., a division of Thomson Learning, Inc.

Lucent Books® and Thomson Learning™ are trademarks used herein under license.

For more information, contact
Lucent Books
27500 Drake Rd.
Farmington Hills, MI 48331-3535
Or you can visit our Internet site at http://www.gale.com

LIBRARY OF CONGRESS CATALOGING-IN-PUBLICATION DATA

Bjornlund, Britta.
    The Cold War ends : 1980 to the present / by Britta Bjornlund.
        p. cm. — (American war library. Cold War series)
Includes bibliographical references and index.
        ISBN 1-59018-209-X (hardback : alk. paper)
        Summary: Discusses the rivalry between the United States and the Soviet Union that led to the Cold War, the actions of political leaders, the U.S.-Soviet summits on arms reduction, the revolutions in Eastern Europe against Soviet domination that led to the end of the Cold War, and the new, friendlier relationship between Russia and the United States.
        1. Cold War—History—Juvenile literature.   2. World politics—1989—Juvenile literature.   3. Post-communism—Russia (Federation)—Juvenile literature.   I. Title. II. Series.
        D856 .B56 2003
        909.82'5—dc21
                                                              2002008590

Printed in the United States of America

★ Contents ★

★ Foreword ★

A Nation Forged by War

The United States, like many nations, was forged and defined by war. Despite Benjamin Franklin's opinion that "There never was a good war or a bad peace," the United States owes its very existence to the War of Independence, one to which Franklin wholeheartedly subscribed. The country forged by war in 1776 was tempered and made stronger by the Civil War in the 1860s.

The Texas Revolution, the Mexican-American War, and the Spanish-American War expanded the country's borders and gave it overseas possessions. These wars made the United States a world power, but this status came with a price, as the nation became a key but reluctant player in both World War I and World War II.

Each successive war further defined the country's role on the world stage. Following World War II, U.S. foreign policy redefined itself to focus on the role of defender, not only of the freedom of its own citizens, but also of the freedom of

people everywhere. During the Cold War that followed World War II until the collapse of the Soviet Union, defending the world meant fighting communism. This goal, manifested in the Korean and Vietnam conflicts, proved elusive, and soured the American public on its achievability. As the United States emerged as the world's sole superpower, American foreign policy has been guided less by national interest and more on protecting international human rights. But as involvement in Somalia and Kosovo proves, this goal has been equally elusive.

As a result, the country's view of itself changed. Bolstered by victories in World Wars I and II, Americans first relished the role of protector. But, as war followed war in a seemingly endless procession, Americans began to doubt their leaders, their motives, and themselves. The Vietnam War especially caused people to question the validity of sending its young people to die in places where they were not particularly wanted and for people who did not seem especially grateful.

While the most obvious changes brought about by America's wars have been geopolitical in nature, many other aspects of society have been touched. War often does not bring about change directly, but acts instead like the catalyst in a chemical reaction, accelerating changes already in progress.

Some of these changes have been societal. The role of women in the United States had been slowly changing, but World War II put thousands into the workforce and into uniform. They might have gone back to being housewives after the war, but equality, once experienced, would not be forgotten.

Likewise, wars have accelerated technological change. The necessity for faster airplanes and a more destructive bomb led to the development of jet planes and nuclear energy. Artificial fibers developed for parachutes in the 1940s were used in the clothing of the 1950s.

Lucent Books' American War Library covers key wars in the development of the nation. Each war is covered in several volumes, to allow for more detail, context, and to provide volumes on often neglected subjects, such as the kamikazes of World War II, or weapons used in the Civil War. As with all Lucent Books, notes, annotated bibliographies, and appendixes such as glossaries give students a launching point for further research. In addition, sidebars and archival photographs enhance the text. Together, each volume in The American War Library will aid students in understanding how America's wars have shaped and changed its politics, economics, and society.

A Dramatic End to an Uncertain Era

The period that marked the end of the Cold War was an exciting and rapidly changing time for those that experienced it. Because the United States and the Union of Soviet Socialist Republics (USSR), often called the Soviet Union, had been principal enemies for over forty years, it is remarkable that today these former rivals look more like partners. For years, each country had tried to outdo the other in a nuclear weapons buildup that not only cost incredible sums of money, but also threatened the entire world with destruction. Yet by the mid-1980s, leaders were working out remarkable agreements to restrict and limit this race. The Berlin Wall, the wall that had separated East and West Berlin for over twenty-eight years, was torn down almost overnight in 1989. That year also witnessed citizens in countries throughout Eastern Europe, countries once dominated by communism, rising up in support of democracy. Meanwhile, the momentum of reform within the Soviet

Union gathered strength and contributed to that country's complete collapse in 1991. No one expected the world to change so dramatically or so quickly.

These changes were monumental not only because they occurred so fast, but also because, for the most part, they were peaceful. There was little bloodshed or loss of life as the world transformed itself. Communist leaders stepped down in East European countries to allow for new, democratic elections. In the Soviet Union, an unexpected turn of events caused General Secretary Mikhail Gorbachev to resign from his post and pronounce the end of the Soviet Union. Although there were isolated incidences of violence or unfortunate deaths, the upheaval of the communist system in Eastern Europe and the Soviet Union came with relatively few casualties.

What Was the Cold War?

The Cold War comprised the period from the end of World War II until the collapse

Germans celebrate on top of the Berlin Wall after tearing down the twenty-eight-year-old barrier on November 12, 1989.

of the Soviet Union in 1991. It featured a political, economic, military, and diplomatic rivalry between the United States and the Soviet Union. Anchored in a clash between two very different ways of life, the Cold War was a competition for power and global influence between the world's two superpowers. After World War II, during which the United States and the Soviet

Union fought together as allies against Nazi leader Adolf Hitler, the two countries found it increasingly difficult to cooperate in the world. As noted by British prime minister Winston Churchill in 1946, an "Iron Curtain" seemed to separate the East, dominated by the Soviet Union, and the West, represented by the United States. This Iron Curtain separated the world for most of the twentieth century.

The mistrust and misunderstandings that characterized the Cold War were the result of two vastly different ideologies. The Soviet Union was a country based on the ideology of communism, whereas the United States believed strongly in the tenets of democracy and capitalism. These two different worldviews clashed over and over again during the Cold War. Soviet communism was a way of life based on socialism that stemmed originally from a German theory called Marxism. Ideally, under communism everyone is equal. Land and property are owned by everyone, while housing, health care, and education are free. The needs of the society as a whole are seen as more important than the needs of any one individual or group of individuals. And in the Soviet Union, it was left to the government to make decisions that would benefit the community. In reality, this meant that the government controlled all aspects of society. It decided who had what job and the price of a pair of shoes. In this system, the Communist Party and the government were one and the same; leaders of the party led the government and the country.

In the United States, a capitalist country, things were very different. Capitalism means that businesses and market forces of supply and demand determine what goods are available in the markets and at what prices. Industries, shops, housing, and land are owned, for the most part, by private individuals or companies rather than the collective whole. And in the U.S. political system, a democracy, citizens choose their leaders by voting in elections that are free and fair. Governmental oversight of everyday life is minimal, allowing individuals to make their own decisions as to what career to pursue or in what town to live.

A Collision of Ideologies

While each system has benefits and drawbacks, during the Cold War both the Soviet Union and the United States viewed the other's system as incorrect and threatening. Both countries worried that the other might one day attempt to spread its

Cuban president Fidel Castro allied with the Soviet Union in support of socialist idealism.

ideology throughout the world. The United States was unwilling to live in a world where communism dominated, and the Soviet Union felt similarly about living under capitalism. Communists tend to believe that capitalism is a selfish ideology as it ignores the needs of the community. According to staunch communist and Cuban president Fidel Castro, "Why believe that the ideals of socialism, which are so generous and appeal so much to solidarity and fraternity, will one day disappear? What would prevail—selfishness, individualism, personal ambitions? That will not save the world; of that I am absolutely convinced."[1] Democracy supporters disagree, arguing that communism stifles the individual spirit. Czech president Vaclav Havel, who lived under communism until 1989 in Czechoslovakia, stated that "[c]ommunism as a system went against life; against man's fundamental needs; against the need for freedom; the need to be enterprising, to associate freely; against the will of the nation. It suppressed national identity. Something that goes against life may last a long time—but sooner or later it will collapse."[2]

The End of the Cold War

There was no exact date to mark the end of the Cold War. Certainly, the advent to power of Gorbachev in 1985 had a major influence in improving communication between the two superpowers. His policies of glasnost (openness) and perestroika (restructuring) produced a momentum for change that could not be reversed. This allowed for the United States and the Soviet Union to improve their dialogue and begin cooperating on nuclear arms reduction. Gorbachev also allowed for another major turning point in 1989: Democratic revolutions took place throughout Eastern Europe as countries rejected communist rule. The symbolic dismantling of the Berlin Wall was another sign that the Cold War was ending. But the unexpected collapse of the Soviet Union, and the subsequent independence of fifteen countries, was perhaps the most significant moment in the end of the Cold War. The Soviet Union, once the principal enemy of the United States in the rivalry known as the Cold War, simply no longer existed.

★ Chapter 1 ★

Reagan and the Final Freeze

Despite the more relaxed relationship between the Soviet Union and the United States that had dominated the 1970s, by the early 1980s tensions between the two superpowers resurfaced. In part, this was due to the hard-line approach of Ronald Reagan, America's new Republican president. A fervent anticommunist since the 1950s, Reagan had little interest in warming to Moscow, and once in office he was determined to maintain his anticommunist crusade.

Reagan, America's fortieth president, ushered in a new era of conservatism and anticommunism in America. Entering the White House in January 1981, Reagan was the oldest president in American history, at only a few weeks shy of his seventieth birthday. American voters had responded well to Reagan's grandfatherly charm, elder statesmanship, and conservative views. During the presidential campaign, he pledged to restore "the great, confident roar of American progress and

growth and optimism."[3] Together with his running mate, former Texas congressman and United Nations ambassador George H. W. Bush, Reagan also promised U.S. citizens that he would lead America in the fight against communism.

Against Détente

As Reagan began to settle into the Oval Office, he made clear that he disapproved of the policy of détente. Détente, a French word meaning the slackening of tensions, originated during President Richard Nixon's administration. It allowed the United States and the Soviet Union to use a more cooperative and less confrontational approach in their diplomatic relations. Détente was an attempt to reach agreements on arms control, trade, and other issues that would allow both sides to live peacefully. President Reagan strongly disapproved of détente because he believed the policy had given the Soviet Union too much freedom and advantage in international affairs. Reagan argued that détente had allowed the Soviets both to build up their weapons and spread communism to other parts of the world while American policy makers looked the other way. Reagan said that, "Détente is a one way street the Soviet Union has used to pursue its own aims."[4] Therefore, the Reagan administration worked to rein in the Soviets.

The New President Rearms the U.S. Military

Believing that the policies under détente had allowed the Soviet nuclear arms capacity to surpass that of the United States, the new president set about to reverse this trend. He wasted no time; in his first two weeks in office he increased the U.S. defense budget by $32.6 billion. In addition, he approved the production of the B-1 bomber, a strategic heavy bomber with the capacity to deliver nuclear weapons and the ability to fly intercontinental missions without refueling. President Jimmy Carter, Reagan's predecessor, had canceled the B-1 bomber program in part because it was considered too expensive. Now, under Reagan, defense department officials at the Pentagon got nearly everything they asked for: an expanded

President Reagan and Vice President Bush meet with other officials to discuss détente.

The B-1 bomber, a nuclear, intercontinental plane, is put into production after Reagan increased the U.S. defense budget.

navy, new aircraft carriers and tanks, and additional conventional weapons. U.S. secretary of defense Caspar Weinberger even announced that his mission was "to rearm America."[5] A new phase of massive military buildups had begun.

President Reagan undertook the largest military buildup in peacetime (the Cold War did not feature any direct fighting between the superpowers) in U.S. history. One of his first proposals as president was a staggering five-year $1.7 trillion defense budget. These spending plans caused huge budget deficits in the United States and often came about at the expense of domestic welfare programs. The U.S. national debt through-

out the 1980s would quadruple from $1 trillion to a startling $4 trillion.

The Evil Empire

President Reagan's military buildup was not the only tool that refroze relations between Washington and Moscow. He used exaggerated Cold War rhetoric, or unsettling language, in which he emphasized that the Soviet Union threatened the safety of the United States. This caused extreme anxiety among Americans. Reagan stressed the Soviet threat in order to gain public support for his unprecedented military expenditures at home. In a televised address on March 23, 1983, for example, Reagan warned the country that the Soviets had a large stockpile of nuclear weapons that could easily strike the United States. Alarming Americans, Reagan asked, "Would the Soviets ever use their formidable military power? Well, again, can we afford to believe they won't?"[6] This kind of tough talk bolstered public support for Reagan's military undertakings.

Reagan also verbally attacked the Soviet Union. The president harshly criticized the Soviets and their motives, calling them cheaters and liars. He said, "The only morality they recognize is that that will further their cause, meaning they reserve unto themselves the right to commit any crime, to lie, to cheat, in order to attain that."[7] Reagan's administration supported these claims often using heightened language as well. Secretary of State Alexander Haig went as far as to warn the Soviets directly that future battles were possible and that the pursuit of peace would not be Washington's priority. He said, "There are more important things than peace . . . there are things which we Americans must be willing to fight for."[8] Naturally, such words did nothing to improve relations, instead they angered and alienated Soviet officials.

Despite the tough talk, Moscow was still open for improved relations. A change in leadership took place when conservative leader Leonid Brezhnev, whose health had been deteriorating for some time, died in November 1982. His position went smoothly to Yuri Andropov, a former head of the Soviet secret intelligence service, known as the KGB. To the surprise of Western leaders, Andropov's first few months in office were marked by a "peace offensive." He repeatedly called for arms reduction and urged a new U.S.-Soviet summit. He proposed nuclear-free zones for parts of Europe and the Mediterranean and a ban on arms sales to developing nations. At a 1983 Warsaw Pact meeting (a meeting that included the communist countries in Eastern Europe and the Soviet Union), Andropov suggested a nonaggression policy for the Western alliance, the North Atlantic Treaty Organization (NATO), and the Warsaw Pact in which all members would agree not to use force against any other member.

But President Reagan was not receptive to these ideas. He remained staunchly conservative and untrusting of the Soviets. In fact, only days after Andropov's appeal for nonaggression, President Reagan gave a speech in which he called the Soviet Union an evil empire. Speaking to an American religious association, he said "I urge you to beware the temptation of pride—the temptation of blithely declaring yourselves above it all and label both sides equally at fault, to ignore the facts of history and the aggressive impulses of an evil empire, to simply call the arms race a giant misunderstanding and thereby remove yourselves from the struggle between right and wrong and good and evil."[9]

Star Wars

A few weeks later, Reagan began to push for a new project that further angered the Soviets. Reagan announced a new nuclear arms program called the Strategic Defense Initiative (SDI). Known as Star Wars, this still-unproven technology involved development of an orbiting anti-missile system that would protect the United States from a surprise nuclear attack. From the start, SDI was very controversial. Critics remarked that the technology, if it were even successful, would be very expensive. Others said SDI violated the Strategic Arms Limitation Talks (SALT) Treaty signed by both countries in 1972. The SALT Treaty

had put constraints on antiballistic missiles as well as intercontinental ballistic missiles and submarine-launched ballistic missiles, all long-range missiles with great destructive potential. The SALT Treaty tried to put the brakes on the spiraling arms race (the long-standing competition between the two superpowers in which each side tried to build up more nuclear weapons than the other).

The Soviets spoke out strongly against SDI. Andropov called SDI "not just irresponsible. It is insane."[10] He added that the Soviet Union would not allow the United States to beat the Soviets in the arms race, stating, "All attempts at achieving military superiority over the USSR are futile. The Soviet Union will never let that happen. It will never be caught defenseless

Ronald Reagan

Ronald Reagan was born in 1911 in Tampico, Illinois. Although a relatively happy youth, he showed little interest in academics. After graduating from college in 1932, he first worked as a sports announcer. By 1937, he decided to try his hand at acting and moved to Hollywood, California. This was the beginning of a successful movie career as he would go on to act in more than fifty movies.

As for politics, the young film actor started as a liberal democrat. In the late 1940s, however, the rising star became active in the Screen Actors Guild where he became involved in disputes over the issue of communism in the film industry. This was Reagan's first formative experience in politics, and it pushed him into the conservative camp. His marriage in 1952 to Nancy

Davis, a film actress and daughter of a wealthy and conservative Chicago doctor, helped to solidify his allegiance to the conservatives.

In 1962, he joined the Republican Party and just four years later, in 1966, he was elected as governor of California. Reelected in 1970, he went on to unsuccessfully challenge President Gerald Ford for the Republican nomination for the U.S. presidency in 1976. In the next election in 1980, however, Reagan successfully won the Republican nomination and was eventually elected to the post of U.S. president. During his first term in office, his anticommunist agenda became an anti-Soviet campaign. Reagan was reelected in 1984 but his second term in office was guided by a more friendly policy toward the Soviet Union.

Third World. The doctrine was based on the notion that direct military, economic, and political pressure against communist movements would put a major strain on the Soviet military and economy. The United States used the Reagan Doctrine as a kind of warning to the Soviets, and quickly showed them that Americans were

by any threat, let there be no mistake about this in Washington."[11] Deeply concerned by SDI, the Soviet leadership became convinced that the United States was plotting an attack. Andropov ordered a worldwide KGB alert in an attempt to uncover any American plans for war. U.S.-Soviet relations were deteriorating quickly.

The Reagan Doctrine

Reagan's anticommunist approach guided his policies toward other countries as well. His policy toward developing countries, a policy that became known as the Reagan Doctrine, aimed to stop the spread of communism around the world. In essence, it pledged U.S. military force and money to undermine and destabilize procommunist or Marxist regimes in the

willing to back their words. In Afghanistan, for example, the United States supplied weapons to Muslim rebels to use to fight the Soviets, which engaged the Soviets in a long, expensive, and draining war.

Under the Reagan Doctrine, aid was also given to countries fighting communism or Marxism in Latin America, which again fueled fury in the Soviet Union. In October 1983, Reagan sent marines to the small Caribbean country of Grenada to overthrow a radical Marxist regime. The program was successful. In Nicaragua, where the Soviet Union and Cuba backed a dictatorial Marxist regime known as the Sandinistas, the United States armed the anti-Sandinista forces, known as the contras. Despite sustained U.S. military and economic pressure, however, Reagan could not bring down the Sandinistas.

Eventually, the Sandinistas agreed to free elections in Nicaragua in 1990 and were defeated.

The Reagan Doctrine was also enacted in nearby El Salvador, where America funded a military dictatorship in a guerrilla war against communist-leaning fighters funded by Cuba. Trying to keep the nation free of communism, Reagan increased the aid to El Salvador's military dictatorship from $36 million in 1981 to $197 million in 1984. Reagan's message to the Soviets was clear: Wherever possible, the United States would work to oppose procommunist regimes. The era of compromise and negotiations achieved during détente was over.

Inside the Soviet Union

In addition to these international problems, domestic issues also confronted the Soviets. The economy, in particular, was headed toward a near crisis state. During the 1980s, the Soviet economy had

What Role Did the Reagan Military Buildup Play in Ending the Cold War?

Many believe Ronald Reagan's massive military buildup, which began in 1981, put severe economic pressure on the Soviets who could not introduce similar measures without destroying their economy. This pressure, some say, caused the Soviets to begin negotiating for reduced arms and this in turn led to the end of the Cold War. Many Reagan supporters allege that this was Reagan's plan from the start, to use a massive military buildup to force the end of the Cold War relationship. Others claim that the plans in the United States had little or no contribution to the changes that took place in the Soviet Union. Ralph B. Levering discusses this debate in *The Cold War: A Post–Cold War History.*

This is likely to be a controversial question among Americans for many years to come, with conservatives and Republicans tending to emphasize the U.S. contribution and with liberals and Democrats tending to play it down. . . . The difficulty in reaching a fully convincing answer is illustrated by the debate in America over whether Reagan's costly defense buildup in general, and the "Star Wars" program in particular, hastened or postponed the end of the Cold War. Several Reagan officials have argued that the buildup convinced Soviet leaders that it would be either futile or too expensive to try to maintain equality with America in the nuclear arms race. Others, including some members of Congress and some scholars, have argued that the buildup postponed the end of the Cold War, partly because the Soviets refused for several years to reduce offensive long-range missiles as long as the United States insisted on its right to deploy "Star Wars" weapons in the future. The most relevant testimony, that of former Soviet officials, is mixed: some affirm that the Reagan buildup contributed to "new thinking" on defense issues and a desire to end the competition in arms, whereas others insist just as strongly that the buildup did not help to end the Cold War.

Armed contras train to fight against the Sandinistas in Nicaragua.

entered into a period of stagnation. This was in part due to the fact that the Soviets were sending military and financial aid to other countries including Afghanistan, Cuba, and Vietnam, as well as subsidizing the economies of its East European neighbor nations. In addition, Brezhnev's massive military buildup, which included greatly increased numbers of both nuclear arms and conventional weapons, had brought the Soviet Union to a level of military equality with the United States, but only at an enormous expense to the country's budget.

Andropov quickly realized that the economy was stagnating and needed re-

form. Attempting to improve efficiency and management, he focused on anticorruption and antialcohol campaigns. In one attempt to shape up the discipline of the average Soviet worker, government agents raided bathhouses (popular relaxation spots that featured saunas and steam baths) and bars to find absentee workers. Under Andropov, the government also cracked down on people engaged in unregistered second jobs known as moonlighting. Andropov also realized that a reduction in nuclear arsenals would free up much-needed finances, thus, his peace offensive was economically motivated.

The U.S.-Soviet Relationship Worsens

Despite any peace offensives, the U.S.-Soviet relationship was deteriorating and in some respects it appeared to have hit an all-time low. In fact, the Soviets walked out of three different sets of arms negotiations. For the first time in twenty years, the two countries were not even discussing how to limit the arms race. The Cold War, it seemed, had been fully revived. Soviet foreign minister Andrei Gromyko stated in September 1983, "[T]he world situation is now slipping towards a very dangerous precipice. Problem number one is to avoid a nuclear war."[12]

The situation worsened further when the United States deployed additional Pershing cruise missiles in Western Europe. Because these missiles had a first-strike capability (meaning that they could initiate a devastating attack), Moscow viewed the move as aggressive. Later that year, in November, a large-scale NATO exercise, Operation Able Archer 83, took place in Europe and concern turned to near panic in Moscow. Moscow worried that an actual initial strike from America would be staged under the cloak of

practice exercises. The NATO exercise put the KGB on special alert. Believing that the U.S. Pershings could reach Moscow in a matter of minutes, the Soviets were convinced that America was planning an attack.

Eventually, this panic was leaked to American intelligence agents and passed on to President Reagan. Reagan was shocked to learn that the Soviets actually

Yuri Andropov developed an economically motivated peace offensive in the Soviet Union.

expected an imminent attack from the United States. He realized that he needed to adopt a new, more appeasing approach. He spoke for the first time about "compromise" with the Soviets, a term not before used in his speeches, and about the need for peace. Speaking at the White House in early 1984, he declared that the year would give way to a new discussion with the Soviets. He said, "1984 is a year of opportunities for peace. . . . If the Soviet government wants peace, then there will be peace. Together we can strengthen peace."[13]

Unfortunately, before Reagan had a chance to meet Andropov face to face to put these promises into action, the Soviet leader died in February 1984. He was replaced by Konstantin Chernenko, an elderly and ailing leader, who had been close to Brezhnev. Chernenko's time in office marked a movement back to the conservative period of Brezhnev and an abandonment of Andropov's economic reform attempts. But Chernenko's term lasted less than a year. When he died, the Communist Party leadership looked within its ranks for a fresh approach to the country's problems.

Chapter 2

Gorbachev and Change in the Soviet Union

The year 1985 marked a new period in Soviet history, a year that would change the country forever. Following the death of Konstantin Chernenko in March, the Soviet Communist Party leadership chose Mikhail Gorbachev, a communist from Stavropol who had been close to Yuri Andropov. Shortly after taking office, the new leader undertook plans to open society and to restructure the economy. These new policies not only brought about unprecedented change in all aspects of everyday life, they also meant improved relations with Western nations. Almost immediately, the interaction between East and West warmed considerably. Although ultimately Gorbachev's reforms would lead to revolutions in Eastern Europe and the eventual demise of the Soviet Union, in 1985 they marked the start of a new era of openness and cooperation. This was the beginning of the end of the Cold War.

A New Type of Leader

After the death of Chernenko, the Soviet Politburo, the ruling body comprising the upper ranks of the Communist Party, met to decide the issue of who would succeed him. Unanimously, they elected Gorbachev. At age fifty-four, almost twenty years younger than the average Politburo member, Gorbachev marked the beginning of a new era. The young Gorbachev was already well known within the Communist Party as an enemy of corruption and inefficiency. He assumed the post of general secretary of the Communist Party and was ready to tackle long-neglected problems.

The new leader understood that the Soviet system was filled with economic, political, and social troubles. Economically, the country was stagnating. The Soviet economy had always relied on central planning, whereby the Soviet central government made all decisions. These decisions included how much of a product a specific factory should produce, at what price the product should be offered for sale, how many workers the factory should employ, and at what salary. Because all factories, stores, land, and other assets were owned by the state, the government controlled all aspects of the economy. This system was proving to be increasingly inefficient and undependable. Many basic goods were not available, and both shortages and long lines for goods were common events. In addition, because many industries employed too many workers and salaries were not tied to performance, workers had little incentive to use their time efficiently. The lack of many goods and the low salaries of workers combined to give Soviet citizens a standard of living that was much lower than in Western countries. These were just some of the problems that plagued the Soviet economy and its people when Gorbachev took power in 1985.

Politically, the Soviet regime was riddled with corruption. Party leaders enjoyed all kinds of kickbacks and bonuses, mostly in terms of material goods. In addition, it was common for a worker in a meat factory, for example, to steal beef and pork to take home. Because certain goods were very difficult to ob-

tain, a large unofficial and illegal market called the black market developed. On the black market, Soviet citizens could get luxury or shortage items that were not available or were difficult to find in the government stores. On the black market, people used close contacts who would find the needed goods and offer them often at a higher price than the item would cost on the official market. Many imported items, including foreign cigarettes, liquors, jeans, and even foreign currency, were obtained by citizens in this manner.

Alcoholism and Debt

The difficulties of Soviet life led to the growing problem of alcoholism. Russians

Mikhail Gorbachev restructured the Soviet economy, improving relations with Western nations.

Mikhail Gorbachev

Mikhail Gorbachev was born in 1931 not far from the city of Stavropol in southern Russia. He joined the Communist Party in 1951 and rose through its ranks throughout his career. He graduated from Moscow State University with a law degree in 1952 but returned to Stavropol in the early 1960s to work for the regional party committee. Elected to the Communist Party Central Committee in 1971, he became a full member of the Politburo, the upper ranks of the party and ruling governmental committee, in 1980. In 1985, Gorbachev rose to the post of general secretary of the Communist Party of the Soviet Union. In this position, he undertook economic and political reforms that were unprecedented in the country. Although he was extremely unpopular among Russians, most Westerners give Gorbachev credit for implementing changes that allowed democracy to rise up in his country and made way for the end of the Cold War. Known in the West as "Gorby," his foreign policy campaign was a great success. He advocated for and negotiated unprecedented arms control agreements with the United States. He was overwhelmingly popular in the United States: In 1988, the term "Gorbymania" was coined to reflect the mood during his visit to America. He was *Time* magazine's "Man of the Year" in 1987, and its "Man of the Decade" for the 1980s. Equally popular in many Western countries, Gorbachev won the Nobel Peace Prize in 1990.

and other Slavic groups had a long history of drinking vodka, in part to help them endure the dreary, cold conditions in the country. But by the 1980s, the problem had grown more serious. This social problem only exacerbated the economic one, as some workers were too drunk or hung over to work effectively. And because of huge defense expenditures under Leonid Brezhnev, the government simply did not have the money to deal with domestic problems effectively. These were some of the challenges Gorbachev faced when he came into office.

Despite the number of domestic woes, even on his first day in office it was apparent that foreign policy issues would also be high on Gorbachev's agenda. In fact, the day after he was chosen as Chernenko's successor, Gorbachev was already talking about the need to put an end to the arms race. This was a priority for Gorbachev because the arms race took money away from solving domestic issues. Speaking to the Communist Party plenum, a meeting of party elites, he denounced the arms buildup and offered the beginnings of a new policy by saying, "We want to stop and not continue the arms race, and consequently propose to freeze nuclear arsenals and stop further deployments of missiles."[14]

The U.S. Response

Although Ronald Reagan had shown little interest in engaging in a constructive dialogue with the Soviet Union for most of his first term in office, in 1985 he reversed his opinion. This was due, in part, to his learning that the Soviets expected an imminent attack from the United States, news that had troubled the president. But more importantly, the Reagan administration was impressed with the new Soviet leader. Reagan had been influenced by British prime minister Margaret Thatcher, who also thought highly of Gorbachev. In December 1984, before Gorbachev became the next Soviet leader, he had traveled to Canada, Italy, and Britain where he met Thatcher, who was immediately impressed with him. In comparison to the older, stodgy leaders who had for so long ruled the Soviet Union, Gorbachev seemed young and dynamic. After the visit, Thatcher told reporters, "I like Mr. Gorbachev. We can do business together."[15] Thatcher's view of Gorbachev made a strong impression on the U.S. president.

Thus, almost suddenly, the United States became receptive to improving relations with the Soviet Union. The Reagan administration correctly believed that Gorbachev would be a different kind of Soviet leader. After six years without a summit between an American president and a Soviet leader, Reagan formally announced that the United States was open

In this 1988 photo, British prime minister Margaret Thatcher listens as Gorbachev (left) speaks of his goals for the Soviet Union.

to improved relations. He declared, "We're ready to work with the Soviet Union for a more constructive dialogue."[16] For his part, Gorbachev was also ready and willing to greatly improve relations between the two superpowers. His immediate priority, however, was to solve domestic problems.

The Need for Economic Reform

For Gorbachev, Soviet economic reform was the primary concern. Despite the vast natural resources of the country in oil, gas, and metal ores, the Soviet Union was not a wealthy country. By 1985 it was struggling economically. The country had stretched itself thin by providing energy and materials to East European countries at very low costs. Its annual subsidy to Warsaw Pact allies, including Poland, Hungary, and Czechoslovakia, was about $3 billion, much of it through discounted prices on oil and other raw materials. Other communist countries also received massive aid from the Soviet Union, including Cuba, who received $4 billion in aid from 1981 to 1984, while Vietnam received more than $1 billion per year. Gorbachev knew that the Soviet finances could not keep up with the new surge in the arms race undertaken by the Reagan administration.

Aid to other countries was only part of the problem. The weakening economy was also an extension of the inefficient system. The central government controlled the production of goods and put emphasis on fulfilling production quotas rather than on the quality of goods produced. This meant that a factory might fulfill its quota and produce a thousand shoes, for example, but all the shoes might be of only one size or color. In addition, the majority of the production focused on the needs of the military. This meant that factories could quickly produce high-quality tanks and steel parts, but washing machines or jeans were not available. The system was dysfunctional, as it did not respond to the needs or wants of its citizens.

Gorbachev offered change. His first step in reforming the economy was *uskorenie* or an acceleration of the economy. The acceleration concept was simple: Soviet citizens needed to work harder and with more discipline for the economy to improve. Gorbachev also introduced the concept of *khozrachet* or self-financing. This policy gave Soviet enterprises more autonomy over their endeavors and demanded that they make profits. However, these reforms produced few results.

Glasnost and Perestroika

In 1987, Gorbachev pushed for a more radical economic reform called perestroika (restructuring). He spoke openly about the Soviet Union's economic problems and reiterated the importance of perestroika saying, "Perestroika is an urgent necessity."[17] Under perestroika, factory and enterprise directors would receive more control to make decisions about

Glasnost Allows Rock Music to Flourish

The following excerpt from Paul Hofheinz's article "Hot, Hot, Hot: Brigada S," describes the new flourishing rock music movement that came about in the late 1980s in the Soviet Union as a result of Mikhail Gorbachev's glasnost policy.

During the Brezhnev era, rock music was carefully controlled through the State Concert Agency, a government bureaucracy that reserved the right to determine which bands could legally perform in public places. Only bands that were officially registered by the agency could receive money for their shows, a ploy that allowed bureaucrats to weed out undesirable groups by choking off their income.

But of course an underground rock scene flourished. Concerts were often a clandestine affair, staged on the spur of the moment in out-of-the-way auditoriums. And despite official discouragement, a few groups like Time Machine, the first band to sing openly about social problems, and the Leningrad-based Akvarium managed to thrive.

When the State Concert Agency relaxed its regulations in 1986, rock bands suddenly could play their music in big halls, with thousands of screaming fans in attendance. The effect was electrifying, and the kids knew whom to thank for the lighter touch. One of the new bands, a Moscow-based group called Grand Prix, introduced a song . . . called simply *Gorbachev*. The haunting chorus ("I understand! Gorbachev!") is less a tribute to the man in power than a defiant youth anthem, undoubtedly the first to use a Soviet leader as an emblem of teenage aspirations.

A rock singer performs on stage in Moscow, Russia.

prices, output, and wages. New laws also allowed for some individual owners to keep a portion of their industry's profits. These were monumental changes in the state-controlled Soviet system.

Gorbachev also introduced a new policy called glasnost (openness). In an attempt to rejuvenate the Soviet society, Gorbachev launched this reform program to release control on the social sphere of Soviet life, in part to jump-start his economic reform policies. Gorbachev believed that economic revitalization would only be possible with relaxed controls on information and decreased censorship. He declared that

> [p]rofound transformations must be carried out in the economy and the entire system of social relations, and a qualitatively higher standard of living must be ensured for the Soviet people. . . . Glasnost is an integral part of a socialist democracy. Frank information is evidence of confidence in the people and respect for their intelligence, and for their ability to understand events for themselves.[18]

While glasnost took shape, the perestroika policy was vague. Some analysts believe that Gorbachev wanted to keep it vague so that he could pursue radical reform while keeping conservatives in the dark. Others believe that he simply did not have a clear vision of how to reform the economy. While he criticized the So-

viet command system that relied heavily on the central government to make all economic decisions, he also rejected the idea of a real market economy (an economy based on supply and demand, as in the United States). Gorbachev, although a reformer, still believed in the communist system. He never sought to abandon socialist principles; he only aimed to reform them. He said, "We are looking within socialism, rather than outside it, for all answers to all questions that arise."[19]

Political Reform Initiatives

Gorbachev believed that he needed new blood in the Kremlin (the buildings on Red Square that housed the government) for his reforms to succeed. Thus, Gorbachev surrounded himself with like-minded reformers. Within a year of taking charge, Gorbachev had removed most of the old conservative leaders from the Politburo and brought in new figures with fresh ideas to help lead the country. This move also helped to attack corruption within the government.

Bringing in new ideas and people sparked a discourse and a range of opinions that had never been allowed among members of the Communist Party. Among these members was Boris Yeltsin, who would go on to become the first president of the Russian Federation. He was brought in as the first secretary of the Moscow City Communist Party Committee, a position similar to the post of mayor of Moscow. With Gorbachev's additions, the party now represented a full spectrum of views and ideas: Some Communist Party members advocated progressive and fast reform while others held more conventional and conservative beliefs.

Mirroring the new pluralism that was now found in the government, a new discourse also began to open up society. Glasnost allowed a greater freedom of expression in the press, sciences, and arts. In June 1986, Gorbachev's team relaxed censorship on literature and other published works. A number of progressive editors were encouraged to run well-known newspapers and journals. Articles with fresh viewpoints on aspects of Soviet history or the Communist Party quickly appeared on the newsstands across the country. Previously censored history books were published for the first time, and émigré works (written by people who had left the Soviet Union to live in other countries) were newly available. In addition, movies never before seen in the Soviet Union were now playing in theaters.

Gorbachev also changed the laws that had limited free speech in the Soviet Union. In 1987, at the plenary session of the Communist Party of the Soviet Union, legislation narrowed the definition of anti-Soviet behavior and propaganda. This resulted in the release of hundreds of political prisoners. Even before this new legislation, Gorbachev had released Andrei Sakharov, a prominent physicist and human rights activist who had spent six years in exile, knowing full

well that Sakharov would continue his campaign calling for democracy and human rights. Sakharov would lead this movement and later pose a great challenge to Gorbachev on such issues.

Gorbachev strove to make the Soviet Union function more efficiently and democratically. His new thinking allowed other groups in society to voice their opinions, and this served to support and further the momentum of change. In addition, because he believed that additional resources were needed to solve domestic problems, he argued for the need to end the arms race.

Changes in Soviet Life

Changes in the Soviet Union were also felt in all aspects of everyday life, including education. In the old Soviet system, lessons had been so centralized and controlled that students in all eleven time zones used the same textbooks on any given day. In 1987, however, the state education policy was being rethought. Many history books were found to be nothing more than Soviet propaganda and were reviewed and changed to reflect a more enlightened view of events. Imagine the shock of students who, in 1987, learned that their final high school history examinations had been canceled because the material they were to be tested on was being revised. History was being reviewed and rewritten!

Such moves had a tremendous effect on society. Whereas during previous eras

Released from exile, Andrei Sakharov speaks to reporters about the need for civil liberties in the Soviet Union.

in Soviet history people were shunned, exiled, or even killed for holding ideas different from that of the central government and Communist Party, under Gorbachev open discussions soon could be heard in every kitchen or café. Sharing opinions no one would have dared express previously, Soviet citizens now debated politics over cups of traditional Russian tea or drinks of local vodka. In addition, the previously controlled culture of Soviet society—meaning that central authorities censored or approved movies and entertainment and the Com-

munist Party owned and edited all newspapers—could now flock to new movies and cultural events and happily read a variety of newspapers and magazines.

Glasnost increased the flow of information, and this allowed Gorbachev to make stronger contacts with society. To solidify support for his reform programs, Gorbachev went out to meet ordinary citizens. Unlike Brezhnev, for example, who

Chernobyl Nuclear Power Accident

On Saturday, April 26, 1986, at 1:23 A.M., an explosion tore apart the no. 4 reactor at the Chernobyl nuclear power plant in Ukraine. The immense explosion and falling radioactive debris caused thirty-one people to die immediately, and thousands were exposed to extremely high radiation levels before they even knew what had happened. In its embarrassment, the Soviet government tried to hide the enormity of the accident, but eventually it was exposed and thousands of people were evacuated from

A photo shows the damaged Chernobyl nuclear plant in Ukraine.

was rarely seen in public, it was not unusual for Gorbachev to visit factories or colleges or to stop on the street to chat with people and talk with them about their everyday troubles. This had been unthinkable during the rigid and controlled era of previous Soviet leaders.

Legacies of the System

Gorbachev faced enormous obstacles in his attempts to reform the Soviet system. For many in the Communist Party, his reforms were unthinkable. Russia had always been ruled by authoritarian means. For centuries, an autocratic czar (an all-

neighboring towns. The accident caused much speculation as to the capabilities of the Soviet system, and it served to spur on Mikhail Gorbachev's reform effort, as explained by Mike Bowker in the following passage excerpted from *Russian Foreign Policy and the End of the Cold War:*

> Glasnost was a theme Gorbachev frequently returned to in his early months in office, but it was only after the tragedy at Chernobyl that glasnost was transformed . . . into reality.
>
> The accident occurred in the early morning of Saturday 26 April 1986 at the Chernobyl nuclear plant near Kiev in the Ukraine. One of the four reactors exploded in what was meant to be a controlled experiment. Gorbachev and the politburo were informed five hours later when the firemen were unable to put out the fire. Three days after the disaster, the whole of the neighboring town, Pripyat, was evacuated. It was the worst nuclear accident in history. Several died in the attempt to control the explosion, thousands have since died from the subsequent radiation fall-out. Yet the accident went unreported in the Soviet media until Swedish authorities detected abnormally high levels of radiation coming from the Soviet Union. Finally, in a small news item on Moscow TV on the evening of 28 April, it was reported that a reactor at Chernobyl had been damaged and aid was being given to those that had been injured.
>
> Chernobyl represented a crisis for Gorbachev and his reform policy. The official delay in announcing the disaster endangered the lives of people who lived in the region. The inadequate coverage after the initial announcement added to a general feeling of panic in the country. The people did not trust their leaders. They certainly did not trust their media. Many tuned into foreign radio stations to try to find out what was really happening. Yet, it was almost three weeks after the accident, on 14 May, before Gorbachev went on TV to give a more detailed statement. . . . He generally tried to downplay the dangers of the accident and criticized the inaccurate reporting of the Western media. More positively, however, he argued that Chernobyl had shown the urgent need to press ahead with glasnost.
>
> [Eduard] Shevardnadze later said, Chernobyl was the first test of glasnost, and it failed. Yet the accident provided an important stimulus for reform. . . . In the circumstances, it became far more problematic for hardliners to resist the reformers' calls for greater openness. Gorbachev later acknowledged that Chernobyl had been "a turning point" in terms of the development of glasnost in the USSR.

powerful monarch) had ruled the country. Since 1917 and the founding of the Soviet Union, all Soviet leaders, from Vladimir Lenin, the founder of communism in Russia and creator of the Soviet state, to the ailing Chernenko, had maintained strict central control. All had been vehemently opposed to any kind of political pluralism, meaning the inclusion of many and sometimes differing ideas. The basic idea behind the organization of the Soviet system was that the Communist Party ruled and oversaw every aspect of life. Its monopoly and dictatorship had remained a stable force for decades. The KGB kept a close watch over Soviet citizens and the state persecuted or exiled those who were suspected of antistate activity.

Reform and the International Sphere

Gorbachev's reforms marked a radical change from the entrenched and politically stagnant Soviet system—including his attempts to improve international relations. His view of international politics was that the Soviet Union should cooperate rather than compete. He was ready to work more closely with Western countries because he realized that the Soviet Union could not both compete in an arms race and successfully solve its domestic problems. Gorbachev understood that finances would need to be freed up and reallocated from defense spending to other programs. With this goal in mind, he aggressively pursued plans to stop the arms race.

In countless speeches, Gorbachev spoke of his commitment to arms reduction. In a speech in Bulgaria, he said, "Nowadays, only our community can prevent a nuclear war. . . . But the complex-ity of today's situation suggests the necessity of finding new steps, new solutions which could lead to the end of the arms race. And the Soviet Union is making and proposing such steps."[20] He reiterated that compromise and cooperation, not confrontation, were needed to move forward, not only in U.S.-Soviet relations, but also elsewhere in the world. "One must not in world politics restrict oneself to relations with just one country alone, even if it is a very important one,"[21] he said. Gorbachev greatly impressed Western nations in 1988 when he made promises that his country's troops would be withdrawn from the bloody and drawn-out conflict in Afghanistan.

The Reagan administration reacted positively to Gorbachev's attempts to resume arms reduction talks. In the summer of 1985, preparations began for the first U.S.-Soviet summit since President Jimmy Carter met Soviet leader Brezhnev in 1979. Gorbachev's ascent to power had changed the atmosphere not only in his own country, but also in the United States. The two countries and their leaders were now poised for open and friendly dialogue.

⋆ Chapter 3 ⋆

U.S.-Soviet Summits Work Toward Arms Reduction

The period from 1985 to 1988 saw a renewed dialogue between the highest powers in the Soviet Union and the United States. The relationship between President Ronald Reagan and General Secretary Mikhail Gorbachev gradually improved through meetings held around the world. Despite vast differences in their political outlooks, the two men forged a successful working relationship that featured better understanding, arms reduction, and new opportunities for trade.

The First Summit: Geneva

Reagan and Gorbachev met for the first time in Geneva, Switzerland, on November 19, 1985. The Geneva summit marked the thirteenth summit meeting between U.S. and Soviet leaders since the Yalta meetings in 1945, where U.S. president Franklin D. Roosevelt, Soviet leader Joseph Stalin, and British prime minister Winston Churchill met to discuss the post–World War II peace. Summits between the United States and the Soviet Union had taken place intermittently over time, but by 1985, a U.S. president had not met a Soviet leader for six years. Much anticipation and hope in both capitals rested on this summit.

The importance of the meeting to the United States was evident by the number of people in Reagan's entourage. As Reagan reviewed his talking points in Washington, D.C., prior to his flight to Switzerland, two hundred members of the White House press corps, forty White House press aides, fifteen Secret Service agents, and approximately ten tons of television equipment took off in a chartered jumbo jet for Europe. In total, 3,614 journalists from all over the world registered at the Geneva summit headquarters.

When Reagan touched down in Switzerland, he gave a short speech on the airport tarmac. He spoke of the "deep differences" between the United States and the Soviet Union, but he added that there was a need for a "fresh start"[22] in relations. A fresh start, despite differences, summed up the essence of the Geneva meetings. Despite being staunchly anti-communist during his first term in office, Reagan now seemed poised and ready to

broker peace between the two superpowers. Gorbachev came to Geneva determined to persuade the American president that he was a different kind of communist leader. In addition, both sides were prepared to discuss possibilities for arms reduction.

A Rocky Start

On the first day of the summit, President Reagan was the official host at the Chateau Fleur d'Eau, a nineteenth-century villa. While their time together without their aides was scheduled for only fifteen minutes, the two leaders spoke for well over an hour. Sitting in a small room in front of a crackling fireplace, Gorbachev and Reagan discussed weighty defense issues. Reagan spoke about the need to create the Strategic Defense Initiative (SDI) as a shield that would protect the United States from nuclear missiles. Gorbachev explained his position: He was strongly opposed to SDI. He even went so far to explain that the Soviet Union would not participate in arms reduction talks if the United States continued its plans to research SDI capabilities.

Reagan (left) and Gorbachev shake hands outside the Fleur d'Eau chateau before the 1985 Geneva summit.

While Gorbachev's main agenda item during the Geneva summit was to get Reagan to agree to stop the arms race, Reagan's main priority was for the United States to continue to develop SDI. Reagan's stubbornness on the issue greatly displeased the communist leader. After the first day of the summit, Gorbachev's impression of Reagan was that his views were outdated. He even told his aides that Reagan was "a political dinosaur."[23]

But by the next day, the tone of the summit dialogue improved. Meeting in the summerhouse not far from the chateau, the two men resumed their discussion on SDI. "We have read everything you've ever said and considered everything you've ever said with regard to SDI," Gorbachev told Reagan. "I think I can understand you at the human level,"[24] meaning that he understood the need to protect one's people, but he added that he simply could not understand or accept the concept politically. Meanwhile, Reagan tried to explain his reasons for insisting on SDI and the need to give Americans protection, stating, "People want defense and they look at the sky and think what might happen if missiles suddenly appear and blow up everything in our country."[25]

But Gorbachev and Reagan could not come to any agreement. After deadlocked discussions on Star Wars, the two leaders walked back to the chateau. And yet, in many ways the real success of the summit happened then. During the stroll, they engaged in a friendly nonpolitical chat. For the first time, they seemed to connect on a human level rather than clashing on a military one. In fact, the chat was so comfortable to both

that Reagan, despite being told by his aides not to mention the issue of the next summit meeting, quickly invited his counterpart to come to the United States for the next summit. Gorbachev accepted. But only on one condition: He stipulated that Reagan had to agree to come to the Soviet Union for a summit after the U.S. one.

Phasing Out the Arms Race

Although it did not resolve the SDI issue, the Geneva summit was viewed as agreat success. The two former adversaries had gotten along well on neutral ground and had established a useful dialogue. They issued a joint statement that avoided the discussion of SDI but that communicated to the world that a new era of cooperation was underway and that the arms race would no longer be a priority. The joint statement concluded:

> The sides, having discussed key security issues, and conscious of the special responsibility of the U.S.S.R. and the U.S. for maintaining peace, have agreed that a nuclear war cannot be won and must never be fought. Recognizing that any conflict between the U.S.S.R. and the U.S. could have catastrophic consequences, they emphasized the importance of preventing any war between them, whether nuclear or conventional. They will not seek to achieve military superiority.[26]

Raisa Gorbachev: A New Soviet First Lady

Mikhail Gorbachev implemented dramatic changes in the Soviet Union in the late 1980s. But it was his wife Raisa Gorbachev who came to embody this new era. The first lady of the Soviet Union during a critical time in that country's history, Raisa was different from former first ladies. She was stylish and smart and she spoke her own mind.

Unlike her predecessors, Raisa had real political power. She traveled frequently with her husband, and consulted with him on important decisions. Mikhail shocked many conservatives in his country when he acknowledged that his wife was politically savvy and influential and even admitted that he frequently discussed politics with her. In the Soviet Union, there was growing resentment among the political elite over Raisa's high profile and influence.

But the West loved Raisa. She first attracted attention from the West in 1984 when she accompanied her husband to England for a meeting with Prime Minister Margaret Thatcher. Raisa's energy and outgoing personality proved that times were changing in the Soviet Union. She greatly contributed to Thatcher's positive endorsement of Mikhail as a man she could work with.

The Gorbachevs were also popular in the United States. When Raisa and Mikhail visited Washington, D.C., for a summit in 1987, Americans were dazzled by the couple. As the pair walked through the streets, excited mobs rushed to meet them. Reporters commented that Raisa's stylish and expensive wardrobe set her apart from the dowdy Kremlin wives of past days.

Raisa's political activities were not limited to advising her husband. The Chernobyl nuclear accident in April 1986 motivated Raisa to work actively in support of children suffering from radiation contamination. This work helped to enhance her reputation at home. Raisa's own health failed in the aftermath of the August coup in 1991. She suffered a stroke, the first of several that would follow, and eventually died of leukemia in 1999.

Mikhail and Raisa Gorbachev visit Washington, D.C., for a summit in 1987.

These topics would be further discussed in future summits.

Not long after the summit, Gorbachev decided that he did not need to wait for the next summit to push forward in arms reduction measures. In January 1986, he proposed the elimination of all nuclear weapons by 2000 and a joint U.S.-Soviet treaty to remove all intermediate-range nuclear missiles from Europe. This would include SS-20s, Pershings, and other cruise missiles. This "peace offensive" proposal was even backed by the Communist Party congress that convened in Moscow the following month. Despite the proposal, American policy makers were skeptical as to Gorbachev's motives. They viewed the proposal as insincere, a political ploy by Gorbachev for international support and attention. American administration officials also noted that even if all the nuclear missiles were withdrawn the Soviets would still be more powerful in terms of conventional arms. This meant that U.S. policy makers still regarded the Soviet Union as a threat to the United States.

The Spontaneous Summit: Reykjavik

While both Reagan and Gorbachev had agreed that the next summit would take place in Washington, D.C., it actually took place in Reykjavik, Iceland. Vacationing in the Crimea, on the shores of the Black Sea, Gorbachev realized that he needed to move forward to refresh the peace process. He needed to remove the stumbling blocks that remained after the Geneva talks. At short notice, and with little planning, the superpower leaders agreed to meet halfway between their two nations, in Iceland, in October 1986.

Gorbachev did not intend to sign any agreements in Reykjavik but he did plan to explain in further detail the need for strategic arms reduction. Because Reagan had made his position clear, that he would not abandon his SDI program, little was expected to come out of the meetings.

On the first day of the summit, Gorbachev began to tackle the arms issue. He proposed comprehensive reductions of strategic arms, including intermediate missiles and space weapons. By the second day, the two leaders had agreed on a "zero option" for intermediate-range missiles in Europe: that is, that the missiles would be withdrawn entirely. A 50 percent reduction in intercontinental ballistic missiles and submarine-launched ballistic missiles over a five-year period was also discussed. Gorbachev escalated the process by proposing full elimination of all ballistic missiles over a ten-year period. Reagan later said, "I couldn't believe what was happening. [I was] getting amazing agreements. As the day went on, I felt something momentous was occurring."[27]

The most dramatic agreement of the Cold War took place almost in a matter of minutes. When Reagan decided to further escalate the agreements by proposing the elimination of *all* nuclear weapons over the next ten years, Gorbachev concurred immediately. It seemed that more progress on an arms treaty was being made in a few hours than had occurred in several years. But before the promise could be finalized, Gorbachev again pushed Reagan on the SDI issue.

Stuck on SDI

The Soviet leader felt he could not agree to cutbacks on offensive arms unless the two sides could come to an agreement on defense weapons, namely on SDI. Gorbachev no longer demanded that Star Wars research be banned completely, just that it be limited to a research project in a laboratory for a ten-year period. But Reagan would not give up his vision of a space defense system. Gorbachev pressed further, mentioning that an arms race in space would be nearly impossible to limit.

They went back and forth, with Gorbachev trying to convince Reagan, and Reagan holding his stance on the issue. The unexpected and historic elimination of all nuclear weapons seemed to be riding on one issue, SDI, or even on one word, laboratory. Each leader tried to appeal to the other's logic and personal considerations. At one point, Reagan hesitated. He passed a note to Secretary of State George Shultz during the meeting that asked "George am I right?" and Shultz wrote back "Absolutely."[28] Reagan would not back down. Eventually, it became apparent to both sides that the

compromise could not be reached. Unfortunately, there would be no agreement to eliminate nuclear weapons.

For both leaders, the breakdown came as a great disappointment. As they walked together outside the meetings, Gorbachev said, "I don't know what else I could have done." Reagan replied, "I do. You could have said yes."[29] But both delegations came to realize the success of the meetings, that the two countries had never before been so close to ending the arms race. Together, in simple face-to-face discussions, they had nearly eliminated the need for nuclear weapons. At a press conference, Gorbachev asserted that the meetings had great significance, saying, "In spite of all its drama, Reykjavik is not a failure; it is a breakthrough which for the first time enabled us to look over the horizon."[30] Only two days later, Reagan agreed that the summit had allowed the two countries to make a historic connection and to move toward real compromise: "The significance of that meeting in Reykjavik is not that we didn't sign agreements in the end; the significance is that we got as close as we did."[31]

The Productive Summit: Washington, D.C.

Gorbachev and Reagan and their administrations continued to negotiate long after the Reykjavik summit. When the two leaders met again in the United States in December 1987, Gorbachev had conceded his anti-SDI position. This was due

A Soviet intercontinental ballistic missile is pictured here. In the mid-1980s summit discussions focused on arms reductions.

to the increasingly dire economic circumstances in the Soviet Union; Gorbachev knew that he needed to secure the end of the arms race and was willing to make major concessions to achieve his goal. Soviet negotiators worked around the clock to put together a detailed and complex treaty that would be acceptable to all. By the time that Gorbachev set out to travel to America, he was ready to sign the treaty, and in the interest of the summit, he vowed to minimize his differences with Reagan.

The summit began ceremoniously with trumpet fanfare and a twenty-one-gun salute. The president welcomed Gorbachev and his wife Raisa to the White House. The official signing of the treaty took place after lunch, and the event was covered live on television. Reagan said, "For the first time in history, the language of 'arms control' was replaced by 'arms reduction.' . . . We can only hope that this history-making agreement will not be an end in itself, but the beginning of a working relationship."[32] Gorbachev responded that the day was indeed significant: "For everyone, and above all for our two great powers, the treaty whose text is on this table offers a big change, at last, to get onto the road leading away from the threat of catastrophe. It is our duty to take full advantage of that chance, and move together toward a nuclear-free world."[33]

The Intermediate Nuclear Forces Treaty

The two leaders sat down at a table to sign the Treaty between the United States of America and the Union of Soviet Socialist Republics on the Elimination of Their Intermediate-Range and Shorter-Range Missiles. Also known as the Intermediate-Range Nuclear Forces (INF) Treaty, the treaty was historic because it eliminated all intermediate-range nuclear arms held by the United States and the Soviet Union in both Eastern and Western Europe. The document required the destruction of 846 U.S. nuclear weapons and 1,846 Soviet weapons within three years. All SS-20s, Pershings, and other cruise missiles would be taken apart and rendered inoperable. The treaty was historic because the Soviet Union and the United States had for years pointed their nuclear missiles at one another in Europe. And for the first time, officials of both countries would be allowed to conduct visits to inspect the missile sites in order to verify that the armaments were being dismantled properly.

The signing of the treaty was not Gorbachev's only success of the summit. Dur-

ing the meetings, his popularity in America skyrocketed. Large crowds of excited Americans swarmed Gorbachev's car as it moved through the streets of Washington, D.C. Gorbachev and his wife even jumped from the motorcade at one point to wave and shake hands with ordinary Americans. The press dubbed America's enthusiasm with the Soviet leader "Gorbymania." Soon after the visit, *Time* magazine named Gorbachev its "Man of the Year."

The Symbolic Summit: Moscow

In the spring of 1988, at the same time that the U.S. Senate was ratifying the INF Treaty signed in Washington, D.C., Reagan was already on his way to Moscow for his final summit meeting with Gorbachev. The Moscow summit was an important diplomatic moment, as Reagan was in his final days as the U.S. president, and he hoped to solidify a good working relationship with the Soviet Union for his successor, President-elect George H. W. Bush.

The summit was also symbolic in that it demonstrated just how far both Reagan as an individual and the United States as a nation had come in changing their viewpoint toward the Soviet Union. Only five years earlier, President Reagan had called the Soviet Union an evil empire. Now he enthusiastically traveled to meet Gorbachev, his comrade, in Red Square in the heart of Moscow.

On May 29, 1988, Reagan and his wife Nancy landed at Moscow's Vnukovo Air-

port. Often drab and cold, Moscow was well prepared for the visit—the skies were sunny and blue, the streets had been cleared of any dirt or debris, and many of Moscow's main buildings had been repainted. Although the first three summits between Reagan and Gorbachev had been in the dead of winter, the Moscow summit took place in springtime and Reagan took note of this in his arrival remarks. In his first day at the Kremlin, he praised earlier summits, claiming that "some of the seeds are beginning to bear fruits."[34]

Gorbachev (seated left) and Reagan smile as they sign the INF Treaty, an agreement to eliminate all intermediate-range nuclear missiles.

The meeting was also important because an American president had not visited the Soviet Union for fourteen years. Reagan's trip seemed to demonstrate that America's long-standing foe might one day be America's friend. Because of his long-standing anticommunist views, Reagan had previously embodied the Cold War attitude of the United States toward the Soviet Union, and this attitude had changed significantly. At the very least, it appeared that the two countries had finally forged a working relationship. According to former *Washington Post* correspondent Don Oberdorfer, "For Americans, the essence of the Moscow summit was the true normalization of U.S.-Soviet relations, not in the technical sense of the formal diplomatic ties . . . but in the sense of accepting the Soviet Union as a 'non-enemy' nation."[35]

Soviet citizens, as well, seemed to have changed their perception of the American president. When the Reagans decided to take an unplanned stroll along the Arbat, an old street of Moscow that was a pedestrian-only zone, Soviet citizens clapped and cheered the Reagans. During his visit, Reagan also gave a speech at Moscow State University, Gorbachev's alma mater and one of the most prestigious universities in the Soviet Union.

Malta: The Seasick Summit

After George H. W. Bush won the presidency in late 1988, he, too, saw the need to discuss arms reductions and other important issues with Soviet leader Mikhail Gorbachev. When Bush suggested a summit meeting place, long negotiations ensued as to the location of the meeting. Gorbachev did not want to travel again to the United States, and Bush did not want to hold the meeting in some neutral country. Eventually, it was decided that the two leaders would meet at sea, off the coast of Malta in the Mediterranean Sea. The meetings were set to take place in December 1989. After the two leaders and their delegations arrived and settled into their respective American- and Soviet-guided ships, a storm began brewing at sea.

The weather deteriorated overnight. The two countries' flags were torn from their masts and scaffolding set up for television crews came smashing down. The next morning it was decided that the seas were too rough for Gorbachev to cross over to the USS *Belknap*, but President Bush was willing to make his way over to the Soviet floating hotel ship *Maxim Gorky*. With the storm raging around them, the two men discussed perestroika, trade issues, and further arms reductions.

After a morning of discussions, the two leaders were scheduled to have three hours of private time before they would resume talks over dinner. Gorbachev's advisors invited Bush to stay aboard the *Maxim Gorky*, but the U.S. delegation returned to the American ship. Television viewers in America watched in shock as their president and his team were whipped by torrential rains and wind as they crossed back to the *Belknap*. The storms closed in and it was clear that there would be no further talks that night. Bush and his advisors spent the rest of the afternoon watching across sixteen-foot waves toward the *Maxim Gorky*. The media reported that the leaders of the two superpowers had flown halfway across the world at a critical moment in history only to be kept a thousand yards apart at sea by a wild storm.

Although the storm raged on the following day, the two leaders managed to meet on board the *Maxim Gorky*. They discussed the momentous changes that had taken place in Eastern Europe and spoke of a new era of cooperation between the United States and the Soviet Union. Despite the hostile weather, it seemed that the two countries left their Cold War hostilities behind at the Malta summit and were moving one step closer toward mutual understanding and cooperation.

Soviet citizens came to realize that Reagan was not an enemy, but an older, stately, even eloquent American gentleman. According to Oberdorfer, "More than any other summit, Reagan's trip to Moscow was a public production that transformed impressions and perceptions."[36]

Gorbachev at the United Nations

About six months after the Moscow summit, Gorbachev gave a speech at the United Nations that was the spark for historic change in Eastern Europe. Despite forty years of Soviet domination, Gorbachev suggested that East European nations should now be free to choose their own form of government.

In his address, Gorbachev spoke of a freedom of choice in international relations and indicated that Moscow would no longer use military force abroad. He declared,

> Force or the threat of force neither can nor should be instruments of foreign policy. . . . The principle of the freedom of choice is mandatory. . . . To deny a nation the freedom of choice, regardless of pretext or the verbal guise in which it is cloaked, is to upset the unstable balance that has been achieved. . . . Freedom of choice is a universal principle. It knows no exceptions.[37]

Because the Soviet budget could no longer sustain supporting Eastern Europe, Gorbachev decided to remove Soviet forces from these countries. He stunned the world when he announced his sweeping plan, a unilateral removal of five hundred thousand Soviet forces, ten thousand tanks, eighty-five hundred pieces of artillery, and five hundred combat aircraft from Eastern Europe. This kind of move was unprecedented and almost unbelievable to East European countries that had been closely controlled from the Kremlin. Real change in Eastern Europe would follow.

Chapter 4

Revolutions in Eastern Europe, 1989

I n 1989, the world witnessed some of the most amazing changes of the century: Democratic and mostly peaceful revolutions broke out throughout the Eastern bloc, that is, countries in Eastern Europe that were dominated by communism. These countries and their citizens, who had been under the Soviet grip of communism for decades, now demanded democracy. Democracy was given a green light by Mikhail Gorbachev, who was planning the removal of Soviet troops from the region. The speed of change was remarkable. No longer backed by the Soviet military, communist dictatorships crumbled almost overnight in Europe. Revitalized citizens regained control of their governments, and by the end of the year, East European countries had turned away from communism and toward democracy. The Cold War was fading fast.

Poland: Solidarity in the 1980s

Poland was a country in the Eastern bloc that had been closely watched by Moscow.

Communism, for the most part, had long been unpopular with Polish citizens. Poland's workers, represented by a political movement called Solidarity, had been at the forefront of the opposition agitating for change—demanding higher wages and better living conditions—since the early 1980s.

Political change, however, did not come immediately to Poland. In 1981, General Wojciech Jaruzelski, a hard-line communist leader, came to power. He strongly supported close ties with the Soviet Union and was ready to introduce harsh measures in order to secure Polish communism. When Poland's poor economy deteriorated further and worker unrest ensued, Jaruzelski acted quickly to defend his regime by imposing martial law, meaning that a strict curfew was put into place for citizens (they had to be off the streets and in their homes each night by a certain hour), the press was closed down, tanks and armored personnel carriers guarded Poland's streets, and all gatherings, except religious services, were banned. Furthermore, Solidarity's leaders, including a popular electrician named Lech Walesa, were arrested.

The state of martial law was very difficult on Polish citizens, and it demonstrated how far Poland's leaders would go to maintain control. But the Polish government could not stifle the democratic opposition completely; the movement went undercover and found support from the Catholic Church in Poland as well as from leaders in the United States. After 1982, when Walesa was released from prison, Solidarity increased its membership and widened its goals, becoming more and more political. As the years passed, Poland's economic situation deteriorated significantly. Inflation soared from 15 percent in 1985, for example, to 650 percent in 1989. This meant skyrocketing prices, long lines for goods, and a real difficulty obtaining needed items. Solidarity demanded a change; workers

Solidarity supporters hoist Polish electrician and future president Lech Walesa on their shoulders. Solidarity fought for the rights of workers.

Lech Walesa

Lech Walesa grabbed national attention in 1980 as the leader of Solidarity, communist Poland's first independent labor union. Born in 1943 in Popowo, Poland, Walesa was the son of a carpenter. He became an electrical engineer in Lenin Shipyard in Gdansk, Poland, in 1967. A strong political activist, Walesa participated in mass demonstrations against rising food prices in 1970 at the shipyard and was later fired because of his protests. Walesa was arrested many times between 1976 and 1980 for his dissident activities.

Walesa's role in dealing with the communists for greater political freedoms won him international recognition and Western praise. When in July 1980 more than one hundred thousand workers striked against raising food prices, the Gdansk shipyards were at the center of the protest. On August 14, 1980, workers seized control of the shipyard and demanded Walesa's reinstatement. Walesa, quickly named their leader, met with Poland's first deputy premier in order to negotiate an agreement to give workers the right to organize freely and independently. In September, Walesa organized Solidarity and was elected its chair. The following year, however, the Polish regime cracked down by disbanding Solidarity and arresting Walesa and several other leaders of the labor union.

Released in 1982, Walesa went on to win the Nobel Peace Prize in 1983, much to the embarrassment of the Polish government. He continued to agitate for reform and was instrumental in bringing about the "roundtable talks" between Solidarity and the communist government. As a result of the talks, Solidarity became a legal movement and was permitted to nominate candidates for the parliament. Solidarity captured ninety-nine of one hundred seats in the senate in the June 1989 elections and a majority of the lower house. Walesa did not run for office himself but later went on to win the Polish presidency in 1989. As president, he led the country through economic and democratic reforms, including privatization and Poland's first fully free parliamentary elections in 1991. Walesa lost his reelection campaign in 1995 to Alexander Kwasniewski, the head of the Democratic Left Alliance. He still remains active in Polish politics.

went on strike, as Poles simply refused to tolerate the deteriorating living conditions any longer.

Poland's government leaders realized that having lost the backing of the Soviet Union, they simply could not lift the country out of its economic decline. Thus, they began to listen to the voice of the people and to Solidarity. In a remarkable move, party leaders invited the illegal oppositionist Solidarity movement to join in "roundtable talks" to take place in February 1989. Lasting for fifty-nine days,

the talks had significant impact. As a result, Solidarity, once an illegal and oppositional movement, was legalized. In addition, free elections were scheduled, and Solidarity was even allowed to nominate candidates for the parliament. The speed and depth of the change in Polish politics was stunning and exciting. Poland's first open elections were held in June 1989, and Solidarity was victorious. It captured ninety-nine of one hundred seats in the senate and a majority in the lower house as well. Later that year, when

Walesa was elected to the post of president of Poland, it was clear that the Polish people had rejected communism.

The Hungarian Revolutions: 1956 Leads the Way for 1989

Hungary had first rebelled against Soviet power in October 1956 when students began demonstrating against Soviet domination. To quell the dissent, the Soviet and Hungarian Communist Party gave the Hungarian leadership position to reformer Imre Nagy. Nagy, however, proved to be too progressive and independent for Moscow and was later removed. With his removal, Soviet troops rolled into Hungary and fighting ensued for the next two weeks. Nearly seven hundred Soviet soldiers and officers were killed and fifteen hundred wounded. Somewhere between three and four thousand Hungarians were killed. Eventually, the uprising was stopped, with two hundred thousand Hungarians fleeing to the West, mostly across the border into Austria. János Kádár, the new Soviet pick to lead Hungary, reimposed strong command over the next few months. The country was again firmly under Soviet control. Nagy, along with three hundred leaders of the rebellion, was later executed.

Despite his initial hard-fisted rule, Kádár mellowed over the years. In 1962, he pardoned Hungary's political prisoners, releasing and forgiving them of any blame. He also instituted impressive economic reforms that greatly differed from how things were done in Moscow. In 1968, for example, Kádár partially decentralized prices by allowing them to rise and fall based on changing costs. Prior to this, Hungary's price policy had been similar to that in the Soviet Union, in which prices were rigidly fixed by the central government. By 1983, a bond market (where citizens purchased official government certificates of debt in return for a loan of money that would reap interest at a later date) was created in Hungary, the first of its type in all of Eastern Europe.

In 1987, an oppositional group called the Hungarian Democratic Forum began to make demands aimed at limiting the control and abuses of the Communist Party. Their demands included freedom of the press, freedom of association, and civil rights. Several other political groups began to organize during 1988 and 1989. As a range of political groups took hold, by the late 1980s it became clear that Kádár's power was on the decline.

The transition to a multiparty political scene rather than just the Communist Party took place simultaneously both within Hungarian society and its government. The Soviet Union, engaged in removing its troops and influence from the whole region, could only watch the events unfolding. Hungarians both within and outside the government seemed to understand the need for change in their country and quickly adopted democratic ideals. In the summer of 1989, the Hungarian opposition organized talks with the communist

government. During these negotiations, communist leaders and oppositional representatives agreed to organize free elections in 1990. Reszo Nyers, a former social democrat, replaced conservative Karoly Grosz as the nation's leader. Hungary's parliament, the National Assembly, dissolved itself and multiparty elections were held in March 1990. In addition, in October 1989, 1,274 delegates of the Hungarian Socialist Workers party formally abandoned com-

Hungarian students surround the demolished head from a Joseph Stalin statue during the Hungarian revolution in 1956.

munism and renamed their party the Hungarian Socialist Party.

The new government quickly ordered the removal of the red star, the symbol of Soviet communism, from all state buildings. The rejection of communism in Hungary had come smoothly and from within.

This triumph of democracy gave encouragement to citizens in other Warsaw Pact countries who were also fed up with communism.

East Germany: The Berlin Wall Comes Down

East Germany was another member of the communist bloc that underwent massive changes in 1989. East Berlin was cut off from its western half in 1961 with the building of the Berlin Wall. This massive concrete structure stretched ninety-six miles through the city of Berlin in order to physically keep East Germans from fleeing into West Berlin. To many people around the globe, the Berlin Wall came to symbolize the separation between the East and West, and its physical presence stood as a stark reminder of the deep political divide that existed in the world.

In May 1989, Hungarian soldiers began to pull down barbed wire fences between Hungary and Austria, "opening the first chink in the Iron Curtain."[38] Thousands of East Germans swarmed through Czechoslovakia and Hungary to escape into the West. When Hungarian foreign minister Gyal Horn asked the Soviet Union if it minded if Hungary opened its border with East Germany, Moscow responded that it had no objections. East Germany, however, objected, as the open

After the Fall of the Berlin Wall

British Journalist Timothy Garton Ash describes the scene in East Germany immediately after the fall of the Berlin Wall in this excerpt from his book *The Magic Lantern*:

Most of the estimated two million East Germans who flooded into West Berlin over the weekend simply walked the streets in quiet family groups. It is very difficult to describe the quality of this experience because what they actually did was so stunningly ordinary. In effect, they just took a bus . . . and went shopping. . . . Berliners walked the streets of Berlin. What could be more normal? And yet, what could be more fantastic! "Twenty eight years and ninety-one days," says one man in his late thirties strolling back up Friedrichstrasse. Twenty-eight years and ninety-one days since the building of the Wall. On that day, in August 1961, his parents had wanted to go to a late-night Western [movie] in a West Berlin cinema, but their eleven-year old son had been too tired. In the early hours they woke to the sound of tanks. He had never been to West Berlin from that day to this. . . .

Everyone, but everyone, on the streets of East Berlin has just been, or is just going to West Berlin. A breathless, denim-jacketed couple stop me to ask, "Is this the way out? . . . Our hearts are going pitter pat." Everyone looks the same as they make their way. . . . But everyone is inwardly changed, changed utterly. "Now people are standing up straight," says a hotel porter. "They are speaking their minds. Even work is more fun. I think the sick will get up from their hospital beds." These are moments when you feel that somewhere an angel has opened its wings.

border had allowed an estimated thirteen thousand East Germans to flee within the first three days. According to Horn, "It was quite obvious to me that this would be the first step in a landslide-like series of events."[39]

In October, Mikhail Gorbachev traveled to Berlin to celebrate East Germany's fortieth anniversary. Throngs of young communists met the Soviet leader chanting "Gorby, save us!"[40] In a speech to the crowds, Gorbachev called for the East German leader and Communist Party chief Erich Honecker to introduce glasnost-type reforms. Journalist David Remnick gives credit to Gorbachev for stimulating East Germany's revolution, stating that "Gorbachev was the man for this moment. In public, he played along nicely with the East German leadership. . . . In private, Gorbachev hinted broadly that the leadership could either begin its own massive reforms or end up defeated and defunct. Gorbachev trotted out one of his favorite aphorisms for the occasion: 'Life itself punishes those who delay.' . . . Such hints can spark a revolution."[41]

Gorbachev's visit was followed with protests against the deeply unpopular German communist regime. Over seventy thousand protestors demanding change marched through the city of Leipzig. But Honecker was not interested in Gorbachev's advice and chose instead to exercise his military muscle. He ordered the secret police to fire on the dissenters. Angered by the use of force, a group in the East German Politburo decided it was time for the Communist Party chief to go. Honecker was ousted and replaced by Egon Krenz, the chief of internal security.

Krenz was young and progressive. He quickly released prisoners from jail and called for "change and renewal."[42] Later, he fired the entire cabinet and two-thirds of the Politburo and opened East Germany's borders with Czechoslovakia to appease the people. Because the situation was still volatile, after consulting Gorbachev, Krenz realized that it was time to open all his country's borders.

On November 9, 1989, Berlin Wall checkpoints were opened. East Germans could freely pass into West Germany for the first time in twenty-eight years. The authorities could not control the Germans who gathered on both sides of the wall to tear down the structure that had separated them for so long. Crowds gathered with pick-axes and hammers to pull down the wall by hand. East and West Berliners tore through opening gaps to embrace one another in a renewed spirit of unity. Songs and celebrations continued throughout the night. The wall that had separated the East and West for years had finally crumbled.

East Germany's communist regime fell in the following year. In January 1990, Honecker was arrested on charges of corruption, misrule, and treason. In March 1990, the East Germans voted out the communists. A few months later, East Germany was the first country to leave

the Warsaw Pact. By the end of 1990, East Germany was dissolved and a reunited Germany was reborn, called the Federal Republic of Germany.

Wielding a sledgehammer, a West Berliner pounds on the Berlin Wall in November 1989.

Czechoslovakia's Velvet Revolution

Czechoslovakia was another of the Soviet Union's satellite countries, a country that like Hungary and Poland had protested the strong Soviet rule. Czechoslovakia experienced a brief period of democratic reforms under leader Alexander Dubček in 1968 known as the Prague Spring. Dubček's goal was to reform Soviet ideology toward a more democratic form of socialism. He hoped to reform an economy

that had been suffering from overproducing heavy industrial goods. In addition, he began to relax censorship on the press, and debate within the country flourished. He called his idea "socialism with a human face." Dubček's endeavors were strongly supported by Czechoslovak citizens, who had participated in a democratic government during the years between the two world wars.

The Soviet authorities, however, began to fear that the Czechoslovak Communist

Party might lose power or that Dubček might change sides in the Cold War. The Prague Spring came to an end when Soviet-led Warsaw Pact troops entered the country in August 1968. Communist conservatives arrested Dubček and other reform leaders and crushed the demonstrations.

The spirit of Prague Spring lay dormant for over twenty years until 1989, when citizens again revived their call for change. On January 15, 1989, thousands of people gathered in Wenceslaus Square to commemorate the death of Jan Paluch, an activist who twenty years earlier had set himself on fire to protest the 1968 invasion. Police broke up the gathering, but unrest grew throughout the next several months. Vaclav Havel, a well-known playwright, and other civic activists were imprisoned. In June, Havel and others issued a statement calling for the immediate democratization of the country. While the government promised economic reforms, it refused to enter into negotiations with oppositional groups as had occurred in Hungary and Poland. Unlike in those countries, Czechoslovakia's government had no reformers within that were willing to push the process. But the Czechoslovak people were encouraged by the successful revolutions taking place at the same time in neighboring countries. This contributed significantly to the government's loss of legitimacy.

The change from communism to democracy took place so smoothly and peacefully in Czechoslovakia that the events became known as the "Velvet Revolution." Whereas in countries such as Poland, Hungary, and East Germany, the revolutions had taken months or many weeks, in Czechoslovakia the country rejected communism in a matter of days. On November 17, 1989, twenty-five thousand students took to the Prague streets to demand free elections. Although riot police came out to disperse the crowds, this use of governmental force only strengthened the resolve of the opposition. Days later, protests numbered as many as three hundred thousand people. When Dubček emerged from years of obscurity to speak to the massive crowd on Wenceslaus Square, the opposition was further invigorated. Dubček demanded the resignation of the government. The resistance pushed further and a general strike paralyzed the entire country on November 27. Finally, the government had no choice but to step down. On November 29 the Federal Assembly removed the clause in the constitution that guaranteed the leading role of the Communist Party. This meant that other political parties and groups could actively participate in Czech life.

At the end of a monumental year, Havel was elected to the post of president of Czechoslovakia, a symbol that democracy and reform had taken hold. In his New Year's Day address, the new president spoke of the new freedom found in Czechoslovakia:

Vaclav Havel

Vaclav Havel, playwright, political dissident, and, later, Czech president, was born in Prague, Czechoslovakia, in 1936. In his youth he enjoyed sports, chemistry, and economics. After serving in the military for two years, he became active at a Prague theater studying stagecraft. During the early 1960s, Havel wrote his first plays, in which he subtly ridiculed the absurdity of bureaucracy in the police state.

As Czech cultural life opened up in the 1960s, Havel began to increasingly criticize government censorship. In 1968, because of these views, he rose to the chairmanship of the Independent Writers Union. After the Warsaw Pact crushed the Prague Spring in 1968, Havel was banned from all theater work. For several years he worked at a brewery in a small Czech town, but he continued to write plays.

After the 1975 Helsinki agreements that included provisions on human rights, Havel wrote an "Open Letter to Gustav Husak," the Czechoslovak party leader, warning him that the regime must honor human rights. In 1977, Havel was a founding spokesman of Charter 77, a human rights group, and because of this he was imprisoned for several months. In 1979, the authorities sentenced him to four and a half years in jail for his opposition work.

Already well-known in the West as a playright, in the 1980s Havel became famous for his dissident activities. In 1989, he helped found Civic Forum, the first legal opposition movement in his country since the late 1940s. Later that year, after the Velvet Revolution had deposed the communist dictatorship, Havel was elected president of Czechoslovakia.

Czechoslovak citizens sing in celebration after the presidential election of Vaclav Havel.

You may ask what kind of republic I dream of. And I reply: I dream of a republic independent, free and democratic, of a republic economically prosperous, yet socially just, in short, of a human republic which serves the individual and which therefore holds the hope that the individual will serve it. . . . People, your Government has returned to you![43]

Bulgaria: The Soviet Ally

Bulgaria, under the leadership of Todor Zhivkov, had long been the Soviet Union's most trustworthy ally. In fact, one popular Soviet joke referred to Bulgaria as the sixteenth Soviet republic. For thirty-five years, Zhivkov would do whatever the Soviet leadership asked of him. Within Bulgaria, he maintained a repressive and militaristic regime. He preserved his control by sending potential opponents to prison camps. In addition, he alienated Bulgaria's Turkish minority, forcing them to take on Bulgarian names to destroy their sense of identity.

In 1989, a number of growing civic groups called discussion clubs signified the beginning of Bulgaria's opposition to the one-party communist rule. Among those active in this movement was Zhelyu Zhelev, a philosopher who had been expelled from the Communist Party in the 1960s because he was critical of it. In 1988, Zhelev was a founding member of the Club for the Support of Glasnost and Perestroika, an informal group dedicated

to implementing Gorbachev-type reforms in Bulgaria.

While it seemed that the Zhivkov regime was solidly procommunist and pro-Soviet, tensions were smoldering both within society and within the communist leadership. In early November 1989, about five thousand people marched on the National Assembly building in Sofia, Bulgaria's capital, to protest environmental pollution. The underlying tone of the march was political as for the first time the people were questioning the ability of the government to improve the environment and the economy. Within the government, the tension manifested itself abruptly. Suddenly, on November 10 a coalition of reform-minded government representatives forced Zhivkov to resign. Unlike the situations in Hungary, Poland, and East Germany, where communist leaders had to give up their power only after confrontations with the opposition, the Bulgarian communists were responsible for removing their own leader. They tried to preempt any opposition by removing Zhivkov themselves with the hope that the power of government could remain in the upper echelons of the Communist Party.

But despite their hope, Bulgarians protested the whole communist dictatorship and demanded the immediate establishment of a multiparty system. After the overthrow of Zhivkov, large street demonstrations took place in Sofia and other Bulgarian cities. On December 13, the

Communist Party Central Committee expelled Zhivkov, thereby signifying a resolute break from the past. According to Politburo member Andrei Lukanov, "[W]e are not only saying goodbye to a person, we are saying goodbye to a policy."[44] At the same meeting, the Central Committee also renounced the communist monopoly on political power.

In the meantime, Zhivkov, formerly the all-powerful communist leader of Bulgaria, was placed under house arrest. Later, he was found guilty of abuse of power and the misappropriation of $3.7 million of government funds and sentenced to seven years' imprisonment. In January 1990, the parliament formally removed the Communist Party monopoly clause from the Bulgarian constitution and allowed for the release of thousands of political prisoners. The Communist Party renamed itself the Bulgarian Socialist Party. Zhelev was elected president the following year. The country had overwhelmingly rejected communism.

Romania: Unrest and Violence

Like Bulgaria, Romania was also staunchly entrenched in communism. But unlike in Bulgaria, Nicolae Ceauşescu, Romania's leader, preferred to rule his country without interference from or consultation with the Soviet Union. This did not make life in Romania more tolerable or open. In fact, Romania was probably the most repressive country in Eastern Europe. Ceauşescu, who became the secretary

general of the Romanian Communist Party in 1965, turned more and more authoritarian and repressive as the years passed. He crushed all opposition to his rule by maintaining a large and powerful secret police called the Securitate.

Ceauşescu imposed hardships on his people that were beyond imagination. In an effort to pay off Romania's foreign debt that by 1981 had reached $11 million, he banned imports and rationed food products. Every product of value was sold for export in an attempt to obtain foreign currency for the state. While Romania's inefficient industries massively wasted energy resources, Ceauşescu banned the population from using more than one forty-watt bulb in any room. During the winter months, people nearly froze to death because heat was available for only a few hours a day. Other aspects of everyday life were equally controlled and difficult; it was even illegal to drive a car in Romania.

Ceauşescu also had a bizarre affection for massive construction projects. Rather than using the money for social programs, he wasted huge amounts of funds razing older, traditional buildings and constructing new ones. The most glaring example of this absurdity was the House of the Republic, a colossal building that covered several city blocks. Its construction required the eviction of thousands of people from their homes and the demolition of eighteen churches and several other historically significant buildings. This project cost the country about $800 million. He also brutally destroyed thousands of unique Romanian villages and forced villagers to relocate into communal drab apartment buildings. Meanwhile, Ceauşescu and his family lived in a number of luxurious homes that included a 150-room villa in central Bucharest.

Ceauşescu maintained a sense of independence from Moscow. He kept the country under totalitarian rule despite Gorbachev's encouragement to East European countries to introduce glasnost-type reforms. Ceauşescu refused to give up his monopoly on power and the riches it afforded him. As other countries turned toward pluralism and democracy, Ceauşescu vowed to preserve the current order, declaring that each country had the right to "decide its own development, path and forms."[45] It seemed that Ceauşescu's authoritarian rule would not be broken easily.

Romanian opposition broke out on December 16, 1989, when thousands of people protested the transfer of a parish priest in the town of Timisoara. Ceauşescu's troops opened fire on the crowd. The shooting continued for several days. Over a thousand people were killed in the events.

Immediately after these unsettling events, on December 21, Ceauşescu organized a pro-government rally. Tens of thousands of Romanians were herded by the Securitate to the front of the presidential palace. When Ceauşescu came out onto the balcony to address the crowd, however, the cheering crowd began to boo and hiss. The usual chants of "Ceauşescu and the people" changed to "Ceauşescu the dictator!"[46] Ceauşescu abruptly broke off his speech and left the balcony; the next day he and his wife fled the city by helicopter.

The movement against Ceauşescu's totalitarian and brutal rule had come quickly and almost unexpectedly. The new government also moved fast to take control, led by Ion Iliescu, a former member of the Romanian Communist Party Central Committee and head of the oppositional group the National Salvation Front. The National Salvation Front proclaimed a commitment to political pluralism and the end to all communist governmental institutions. According to analyst Vladimir Tismaneanu, "the Romanian Communist party seemed to disappear as if it had never existed."[47]

Unfortunately, the revolution in Romania did not take place as smoothly or peacefully as had the revolutions in the rest of Eastern Europe. Two days after fleeing the capital of Bucharest, Nicolae and Elena Ceauşescu were captured. On Christmas Day, 1989, after a nine-hour trial, they were found guilty of genocide. The couple was immediately put to death by firing squad. Their bodies were shown to the public on Romanian television and the pictures were broadcast throughout the world. With this dramatic scene, communist control in Eastern Europe was extinguished. The Cold War itself was nearly over.

At the start of 1989, the Iron Curtain had divided Eastern and Western Europe. Within a year, popular citizen uprisings had ousted nearly every communist leader in Eastern Europe. The change that took place was simply remarkable. The fact that revolutions took place in a number of different countries so quickly and, with the exception of Romania, practically without bloodshed was absolutely amazing. The will of the people had overcome all obstacles. The Cold War buffer zone that the Soviets had fortified in Europe had vanished. The Soviet Union itself might now be vulnerable to democratic change.

Chapter 5

Challenges to Communism Within the Soviet Union

As communism collapsed in Eastern Europe, Mikhail Gorbachev found communism challenged from within the Soviet Union as well. The entire Soviet system was suffering profound stresses that included a rapidly changing political society, the deep need for economic reform, the strengthening of grassroots and nationalist movements, and a struggle within the Communist Party between conservatives and reformers.

Political Pluralism and the Congress of People's Deputies

In the late 1980s, pluralism, or the appearance of a variety of different political viewpoints in society, was evolving rapidly in the Soviet Union. Gorbachev's reforms had stimulated the formation of new political groups and organizations. New journals and newspapers emerged as did new discussion clubs called "informals." Informals featured people getting together in cafés or universities to discuss a

certain political issue or idea, an activity that previously had been strictly regulated. Other groups came together around the issue of political dissidents, meaning people who were exiled and sent to live in undesirable parts of the country because of their political views or actions. In addition, groups called popular fronts began to take on political agendas that included increased autonomy over their own affairs. These new groups gained significant momentum as Gorbachev's political reforms unfolded.

One of Gorbachev's most progressive and sweeping political reforms was the creation of a new legislative body, the Congress of People's Deputies. This new legislature was a large body with 2,250 deputies, and two of the three chambers would be directly elected by the Soviet people. (The third chamber of the congress was made up of seats reserved for the Communist Party of the Soviet Union and other Soviet organizations). The main duty of the Congress of People's Deputies was to elect a Supreme Soviet— a smaller body of 542 members that would have most of the lawmaking powers. According to the newly amended constitution, the Supreme Soviet could initiate and review legislation. In addition, a Commission of Constitutional Review, a kind of supreme court, was also created to oversee the workings of the congress. The new system called for candidates to be elected through secret ballots, and for the first time in Soviet history voters had a real choice among a number of candidates. In addition, for the first time, candidates who were not members of the Communist Party could run. The first historic election to this body took place in March 1989.

The March elections were a turning point in Soviet history. This was the first time that noncommunists were given a voice in government. While 80 percent of the winning candidates were Communist Party members, significantly, 20 percent were not. Many new political groups and

The Congress of People's Deputies convenes in the Kremlin to elect a Supreme Soviet.

players came to the foreground during these monumental elections. And remarkably, even if there was only one candidate running, voters had the opportunity to reject that candidate by crossing his name off the ballot. This occurred in Leningrad: Party chief and Politburo member Yury Solovyev was not elected when 130,000 people crossed his name off the list while only 110,000 had voted in favor of him.

A New Era of Choice

Signifying the start of a new era, the congress gave citizens a new, unprecedented voice in choosing their government. Prior to this, elections had been a mandatory show of support for candidates selected by the communist government. Voters had been required to come to the polls to circle candidates' names. To refuse to do so was not looked on favorably by the government and secret police. Thus, the Soviet Union boasted a high voter turnout, although, in essence, the voter had no real choice. Now, elections actually gave the citizen a real vote and a choice that included noncommunists. A sense of excitement was in the air.

The congress was historic also because for the first time in Soviet history its meetings were broadcast on television. Suddenly, people became extremely interested in politics. Millions of viewers were glued to their television sets to watch the legislative and political debates unfold. Informals began to hold rallies to in-

fluence the agenda of the new congress. In Moscow, this developed into large and recurring gatherings. At the end of the working day, tens of thousands of people came out regularly to the Luzhniki sports stadium where their congressional deputies met them. The deputies spoke to the crowds and reported on the day's proceedings at the congress. This contact between the people and their elected deputies—between citizens and government—was direct and unprecedented in the Soviet Union. People had a new and healthy interest in politics.

Having created the new legislature, Gorbachev initially used it to consolidate and increase his own power. When the congress met for the first time in late May to elect its Supreme Soviet, the Supreme Soviet named Gorbachev its president. Gorbachev now was both general secretary of the Communist Party of the Soviet Union and president of the Supreme Soviet of the Soviet Union. Domestic critics accused him of taking too much power for his own aims. A Moscow journalist wrote, "From now on Gorbachev is to be President, the parliament, the government and the ruling party simultaneously."[48]

Economic Failures

Political successes, unfortunately, were not accompanied by economic ones. Achievements and breakthroughs in the political arena were taking place against the backdrop of a severely deteriorating economy.

The Soviet budget deficit was growing; despite Gorbachev's calls to reduce military spending, it continued to rise until 1989, creating a huge drain on the economy. Also, while Gorbachev had instituted a number of needed social programs, they came at additional cost to the Soviet budget. He raised pension payments for the first time since the 1950s, for example, and began an ambitious housing program. He initiated an antialcohol campaign that meant reduced income for the government, the recipient of any profits from alcohol sales. The budget was further hurt by a drop in oil prices in the mid-1980s, as

A young girl who lives in a tent city stands outside her home behind the Kremlin. Some Soviet citizens set up and lived in tents to protest the declining standard of living.

oil was the country's most lucrative and abundant export.

The economy also suffered declines in productivity and output that meant fewer goods and a lower standard of living. Because the central government had controlled all aspects of economic production, companies had little interest in reducing their costs or working efficiently. Productivity, often measured in the amount each worker can produce, was extremely low as compared to the United States. In 1980, an American farmer produced enough to feed sixty-five people per year, while in the Soviet Union one farmer only produced enough to feed six people. By 1990, the Soviet economy showed continued declines in nearly every sector—the total production of both industrial and agricultural goods was decreasing.

Tough Times

The lack of Soviet goods and the inability to buy foreign ones meant that life was extremely tough for average citizens. Because shortages of normal goods had become customary, most Soviet citizens bought more than they needed and stored the extra goods at home. Soviet apartments and balconies were usually stuffed with all kinds of products to help people get through future tough times. This mass buying and hoarding of available goods produced and further exacerbated shortages. As an article in *Time* magazine explained the difficult situation, "day-to-day life in the Soviet Union is as difficult as ever. Not only are big consumer items like refrigerators and washing machines in short supply—the average wait to buy the cheapest Soviet car is seven years—but staples of everyday life are also scarce. Long lines snake into the street for such ordinary items as sausage, rice, coffee and candy."[49]

Despite all of Gorbachev's attempts to reform the Soviet Union, ironically, his reforms were now part of the economic problem. Forced by Gorbachev to become financially profitable, yet with little understanding of how this is done, Soviet industries were producing fancier products at higher prices. Consumers, for example, were unable to buy regular soap at the usual price of about 32 cents a bar because factories were only producing a luxury type of soap for $1.60 a bar. This price was too high for the regular consumer and both consumer and producer lost; the people could not buy any soap and the factories did not make any money because they had not sold their product.

Although the Soviet leader was extremely concerned about the still-deteriorating economy, the entrenched system was resistant to change. Rebuilding the economy proved far more problematic than Gorbachev had ever expected. Speaking to the Communist Party, he admitted this: "Frankly speaking, comrades, we have underestimated the extent and gravity of the deformations."[50] Because the economy had been in a stagnant or even deteriorating state for so long, reversing this trend to build a healthy, growing economy was nearly impossible. Nikolai Shmelev, a well-known Russian scientist and economist, spoke colorfully about the economy, explaining in 1989, "We are now like a seriously ill man who, after a long time in bed, takes his first step with the greatest degree of difficulty and finds to his horror that he has almost forgotten how to walk."[51]

Trying to Change

Now, with his expanded political powers, Gorbachev tried again to solve the country's financial woes. He decided to jump-start the economy by moving from a planned and central system to one that relied increasingly on the market, a system of supply and demand like in most Western countries. In April 1990, he announced that new, sweeping market-oriented reforms were planned. This meant that rather than relying solely on the central government to impose production decisions and prices, the individual citizen or individual company would start to have a say in the economy. In a market economy, if the people demand more pasta, for example, its price goes up and this in turn stimulates the factory to produce more and increase supply. With these aims, Leonid

In this 1991 photo, a Russian woman walks past well-stocked produce stands. At the time, food was extremely expensive in the Soviet Union, where the economy was severely depressed.

Abalkin, Gorbachev's economic advisor, outlined a new economic refrain package that included privatization, that is, moving assets such as factories and shops from government to private ownership, as well as aspects of banking and tax reform. But the plan barely got off the ground.

When the official reform program was launched on May 23, Soviet prime minister Nikolai Ryzhkov announced that major increases in prices would take place by July 1. Prices would be allowed to increase in order to reflect the actual costs of manufacturing the product. When Ryzhkov mentioned that the price of bread would triple, Soviet citizens panicked. The government had always heavily subsidized the price of bread, and consumers were accustomed to buying bread products at rock-bottom prices. Worried about the new price hikes, people flooded the stores and bought up massive quantities of bread. Bread shortages followed. Displeased with these results, the Supreme Soviet rejected the economic reform package. Gorbachev's advisors would have to return to the drawing board to try to find other ways to revive the struggling Soviet economy.

The Rise of Nationalism

When Gorbachev came into power in 1985, he not only inherited a country with a deteriorating economy, he also inherited one filled with erupting national tensions. These tensions became one of the greatest challenges to communism within the Soviet Union.

The Soviet Union was a huge multi-ethnic country with over 170 different ethnic groups. To cope with the challenge of the great number of different nationalities and ethnic groups, the Soviet Union had been created as a federation of fifteen republics, and within each were smaller autonomous republics, as well as provinces, districts, and regions. As glasnost opened up the political system, it gave ethnic or nationalist groups a new opportunity to examine their heritage and express their culture. Interest in one's ethnicity meant various things. For some groups it meant discovering old languages and cultural traditions; for others it meant asserting their republic's sovereignty or independence; and for still others it led to ethnic violence. In all cases, severe pressure was put on the country to stay unified and on the central government that struggled to contain it.

The Baltic Republics Revolt

Because of their location and history, the Baltic peoples were poised to take advantage of the more open society that was being created under Gorbachev. As in other Soviet republics, new reforms allowed the Balts to celebrate their ethnic heritage. Flags and badges appeared everywhere with the Estonian, Latvian, and Lithuanian emblems. Song festivals, where people met to sing ethnic songs in their native languages, became enormously popular. In addition, the revival of the

Thousands of Lithuanians fill the streets to protest for independence from the Soviet Union.

Baltic churches also led to a renewed feeling of national self-awareness.

By 1988, groups called popular fronts were established in each of the three Baltic republics. Popular fronts were not political parties. They were instead groups of reformers that included members of the Communist Party and the government who were ready to put nationalism, that is, the loyalty, patriotism, and aspirations of their people, as their first priority. When Gorbachev's reforms allowed for popular front candidates to run for the new Congress of People's Deputies, these Baltic nationalist groups gained further strength. Within the context of these historic elections, Baltic popular front candidates did extremely well at the polls. While Communist Party members still held the majority of seats, the popular fronts had strengthened their positions and their demand for change.

At first, the democratic victories of the popular fronts provided exactly what Gorbachev had hoped for: a new thrust for reform in the most economically and politically advanced part of the Soviet Union—the Baltic republics. He hoped that the Baltics might quickly become the model of reform for the rest of the country. Thus, initially, he supported their aims, including their calls for more control over their own economies and for greater cultural awareness. But Gorbachev soon understood that he had underestimated the resolve of the Baltics as the popular fronts moved beyond their initial demands and began speaking of sovereignty or even independence from the Soviet Union.

The issue that contributed most to the rapid rise in nationalism in the Baltic republics was the protest against their forcible integration into the Soviet Union in 1940. The Baltic peoples believed that their incorporation into the Soviet Union had been illegal. Therefore, in 1989, on the fiftieth anniversary of the Nazi-Soviet pact of 1939 (the pact between Joseph Stalin and Adolf Hitler that had allowed for the incorporation of the Baltic republics into the Soviet Union), 2 million Balts linked hands across three republics to protest their inclusion in the Soviet Union. The boldness and political sentiment behind this human chain gave Gorbachev and other leaders a glimpse of the anti-Soviet sentiment in the region. For the first time, he spoke out against the Baltic movement, criticizing its "nationalist excesses." He even went on to threaten the movement's members by claiming that "the state of all Baltic peoples is in serious danger."[52]

Lithuania moved first to rebel against Moscow's control. In December 1989, the Lithuanian Communist Party voted to become an independent Communist Party from that of the Soviet Union. The Kremlin called the move illegal. Then in March 1990, the Lithuanian Supreme Soviet (a republic-level legislative council) declared Lithuania an independent state

The Nazi-Soviet Pact and the Baltic Republics

In 1939, just before the start of World War II, officials from Nazi Germany and the Soviet Union signed a pact in which they declared that neither country would attack the other. The pact included a secret protocol in which the two countries assigned regions of influence in Eastern Europe. This secret pact allocated control of the independent Baltic states of Estonia, Latvia, and Lithuania to the Soviets. However, Adolf Hitler did not keep his promise of nonaggression, invading Soviet territory only two years later. Anticipating this, the Soviets had stationed Soviet Red Army forces within the borders of the Baltics in 1939. About a year later in 1940, the Red Army forcibly annexed the region to the Soviet Union.

Among the countries of the former Soviet Union, the Baltic countries have had the smoothest transition into independence. Democracy and a free market have been easier to set up in part because all three countries have long-standing ties with the West. Historically, Lithuania has been strongly influenced by Poland, and Latvia and Estonia have close ties to Germany and Scandanavia. The small Baltic countries are more urbanized than most other parts of the former Soviet Union and enjoy a high standard of living.

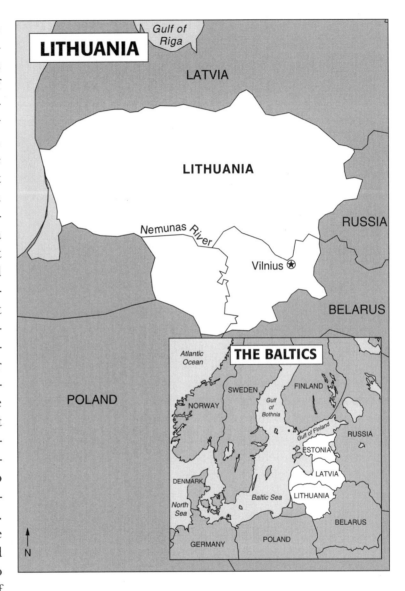

and part of Europe. The Lithuanian Soviet Socialist Republic changed its name to the Republic of Lithuania and a president and prime minister were quickly appointed. By March 30, 1990, the Estonian Soviet Socialist Republic made its own declaration of independence, and in May, Latvia followed. Claiming that the Baltic republics had been illegally incorporated into the Soviet Union, Lithuanian president Vytautas Landsbergis had explained their position only a year earlier, declaring, "We are not part of the Soviet Union under international law. The annexation of 1940 gives no legal grounds for us being in the Soviet Union. We are a part in some practical way, we are ruled from Moscow. But we do not feel ourselves part of the Soviet Union."[53]

Probably to appease party conservatives, Gorbachev's administration reverted to handling problems in the ways of the old Soviet regime—by using force to keep nationalist outcries in check. In January 1990,

when ethnic rioting broke out in the Republic of Azerbaijan, Gorbachev sent in troops, and as many as a thousand people were killed. When Lithuania declared its independence from the Soviet Union, Gorbachev did not use force although he did call the move "illegitimate and invalid."[54] He also instituted an economic embargo. He cut off oil supplies and over 80 percent of the flow of natural gas, letting through only enough to keep essential places, such as hospitals, running. How far Gorbachev would go was unclear. It seemed that he had abandoned supporting the views of his people, views once welcomed by glasnost. After stoking the fires of democracy, Gorbachev now had reversed his position and was supporting the views of communist conservatives over that of the people.

The Domino Effect: Other Republics Declare Sovereignty

The Baltic fever inspired other ethnic groups to gain confidence to stand on their own. In Moldova, people demanded the republic's reunification with Romania. Armenia asserted its right to veto Soviet laws. Similar to the claims of the Baltic republics, the Georgian Supreme Soviet openly condemned the forcible occupation of its territory in 1921 and its incorporation into the Soviet Union. In Ukraine, the nationalist Rukh movement gained significant popularity not only in western Ukraine (which was annexed to Soviet Union in 1939), but also in cities in central Ukraine. The Ukrainian flag appeared, in some cases replacing the Soviet one. Nationalism was on the rise.

The Decline of Communism

Communism was on the decline in the Russian republic as well. In February

1990, over 2 million people gathered in Moscow to demand an end to the Communist Party monopoly. A few weeks later, Gorbachev proposed exactly that: a new multiparty system rather than a system based solely on the Communist Party. On March 13, the Congress of People's Deputies agreed; in a vote of 1,771 to 24, article 6, which guaranteed the leading role in government to the Communist Party, was deleted from the Soviet constitution. This deletion of article 6 was historic; it meant that for the first time in over seventy years other political parties and movements could now legally participate in Soviet politics (independents— that is, candidates without any specific party affiliation—had been allowed to run for some of the seats in 1989).

While deflating the role of the Communist Party, the congress further boosted the role of Gorbachev. At the same March session, the congress voted to increase the power of the presidency, and two days later it elected Gorbachev as Soviet president for a five-year term. The congress also approved Gorbachev's idea to create a presidential council, which in essence replaced the Communist Party Politburo, and a federation council, in which heads of each republic would be represented. This seemed to be a major political boost for Gorbachev. He had responded to the wants of democratic reformers by securing the vote against Article 6, while also enhancing his own power and prestige. Things were changing rapidly, and for

68

the time being Gorbachev was successfully walking a thin line between conservatives and reformers.

Gorbachev's Successes Abroad: The Cold War Winds Down

Despite the difficulties at home, Gorbachev's reputation was soaring abroad. In a June summit between the United States and the Soviet Union, the new U.S. president, George H. W. Bush, and Gorbachev signed agreements dealing with chemical and nuclear weapons. Gorbachev also accepted the reunification of

Germany and that country's entrance into the North Atlantic Treaty Organization (NATO), an issue that Gorbachev had earlier thought threatened Soviet security.

On October 3, 1990, Germany officially reunified, and it seemed that another famous symbol of the Cold War had disappeared. Then, in November 1990 the United States, the Soviet Union, and thirty other nations met to sign the Charter of

Gorbachev extends his hand to U.S. president George Bush during a 1990 summit.

Paris, an official document that many said meant the end of the Cold War. The charter included a nonaggression pact between NATO and the Warsaw Pact.

While the world was becoming a safer place and it seemed that the Cold War was winding down, Gorbachev still had an uphill battle in front of him. He had been unable to solve his country's economic problems. His political reforms had allowed for new groups to rise up, groups that now threatened to destroy the system entirely. Gorbachev sensed his declining political influence as the demands of the republics grew. His challenge would be not only to preserve his own position as Soviet leader, but also to preserve his country.

Chapter 6

The Struggle to Preserve the Soviet Union

The Soviet Union was now struggling to cope with competing problems all of which threatened the country's cohesiveness. The Soviet leader was trying, against all odds, to reform a deteriorating and inefficient economy while also attempting to open a political system resistant to change. In addition, the rise of nationalism and the popularity of independence in the republics threatened to rip the Soviet Union apart. As the momentum of nationalism spread, even the loyal Russian republic was affected.

The Rise of Boris Yeltsin

Once a fellow communist, Boris Yeltsin had broken with Soviet ranks in 1987 when he criticized the Soviet system and was let go as the leader of the Moscow Communist Party. After renouncing communism completely, Yeltsin was elected to a seat in Russia's newly created Congress of People's Deputies. In May 1990, he was chosen by its Supreme Soviet as chairman, which, in effect, gave Yeltsin the highest political position in the Russian republic. Now, Yeltsin was using his power and his increasing popularity to push for the needs of the Russian people. Promoting the rights of Russia, a part of the Soviet Union, Yeltsin posed a threat to Mikhail Gorbachev, the Soviet leader.

Yeltsin began to defy official Soviet policy almost immediately. Only days after becoming the new leader of Russia, he met with the new leader of Lithuania, the Soviet republic that had recently declared its independence from the Soviet Union. The meeting was a slap in the face of Gorbachev who refused to recognize Lithuania's independence. Such challenges continued as the Russian Supreme Soviet declared that its laws would take precedence over Soviet ones. Because Russia had traditionally been the core of the Soviet Union, this move was highly threatening to Gorbachev and other central

Gorbachev (center) sits next to Boris Yeltsin during the 1990 session of the Congress of People's Deputies.

figures. According to historian Raymond L. Garthoff, "It was one thing if one or even all of the small, peripheral Baltic or Transcaucasian republics avowed sovereignty or even sought to secede; it was quite another for Russia to declare the primacy of its government over the territory and resources of most of the country in a direct challenge to the legitimacy of the Soviet central government and state."[55]

The Soviet central government was increasingly threatened as Yeltsin's power and influence grew. Seven other repub-lics followed the lead of Russia and declared the sovereignty of their republic's laws over the laws of the Soviet Union. Recognizing that his political power was waning, Gorbachev proposed a new central government that comprised representatives from all fifteen Soviet republics. But Yeltsin, whose popularity and confidence were growing, refused to back this plan.

The relationship between the Soviet government led by Gorbachev and the Russian government led by Yeltsin grew tenser. According to historians Jeremy Isaacs and Taylor Downing, "A fork in the road had come clearly into view: one branch pointed toward Gorbachev and a restructured Soviet Union; the other towards Yeltsin and Russia, and the dissolution of the Soviet Union."[56]

Gorbachev Fluctuates Between Conservatives and Reformers

Gorbachev was stuck between nationalist movements in the republics and communist conservatives in the Soviet government. To appease nationalists, he proposed a new Union Treaty that foresaw a union of sovereign republics with loosened ties between the republics and the central government. Gorbachev's proposal was not well received by Communist Party conservatives, who feared that he was giving away their power. Facing pressure from these hard-liners, toward the end of 1990 Gorbachev altered his strategy. He brought archconservatives back into the government. He fired a moderate interior minister and replaced him with Boris Pugo, the conservative former KGB chief in Latvia. Gorbachev explained the decision in antinationalist terms saying, "The country needed firm executive rule to overcome the threat posed by the dark forces of nationalism."[57] In a move that shocked many but seemed to prove that Gorbachev had abandoned reform, Soviet

foreign minister Eduard Shevardnadze resigned in December warning that authoritarian forces were overtaking the central government. Shevardnadze said, "I firmly believe a dictatorship is approaching. No one knows what sort of dictatorship, or who the dictator will be."[58]

Gorbachev's shift away from reform had some unfortunate results when he allowed the use of brute force in the Baltics. As Lithuania continued its plans for independence, on January 10, 1991, Gorbachev first threatened to impose presidential rule. He claimed that the situation had gotten out of control and asserted that the people called for a strong hand to resolve the situation and for the restoration of order and the establishment of presidential rule. The situation escalated when Soviet troops and riot police seized state-owned buildings in Vilnius, Lithuania, and Riga, Latvia. Sunday, January 13, 1991, became known as "Bloody Sunday," when Soviet forces stormed the television tower and other buildings in Vilnius. The scene was dangerous, according to a Lithuanian woman who gave the following personal account of the scene: "Some people tried to push the tank back with their bare hands. My legs got tangled. I stumbled and fell on my back. I felt the tank treads pressing on my legs. I didn't feel great pain. But I was shouting very loudly, with all my strength, 'Mama.'"[59] Fourteen people died in the event. The following Sunday, Soviet troops attacked the Interior Ministry in Riga, killing five Latvians.

First-Hand Account of Bloody Sunday

The following is the personal account of Lithuanian citizen Virgilijus Skulskis who was working at Lithuania's parliament building during the period leading up to Bloody Sunday. Taken from an August 2002 interview conducted by the author, Skulskis reported the following.

> One of our leaders came up with the idea to defend the main parts of our Republic. And so it began before the New Year. We created a human chain of people that was surrounding the Supreme Soviet building, the Parliament. The human chain protected our building day and night. They lit campfires to stay warm. Everyone was concerned but happy—we were defending our heart—the cradle of the Republic.

> At first the barricades appeared at the Parliament building. They were put up at all the entrances; there was only one narrow entrance for cars.

> Our human chain welcomed people from all parts of the Republic. All types of people arrived, many of the elderly prayed. A member of the agricultural committee, I was in the Parliament building working, but at times I enjoyed coming out to the square to talk with my fellow Lithuanians. There was a sense of purpose and euphoria there. In these moments, we were storing energy for what lay ahead. And inside the parliament, we were working intensively getting ready for anything. People brought sandbags to protect the building; the roof was prepared with barbed wire; iron grids were put inside

> and outside the building. When we entered the building our documents were closely checked and we were given gas masks. We were told to keep the light low, at day or night. At some point, I realized the danger of the situation and that there would be bloodshed. The tension grew everyday. Medical supplies and guns were dispersed.

> A few days before Bloody Sunday, our fighters swore their allegiance to the Republic of Lithuania. Young children and women were recommended to return home as we prepared for the worst.

> Then one night during the second week of 1991, it began. A large column of tanks and armored personnel carriers began pushing to the center of the city. They passed our parliament building, where we were terrified, and stopped at the radio and television station.

> The storm command was issued. Tanks began firing blanks first to scare the crowd. Then they began to attack and started firing real bullets. They hit unarmed, defenseless people and pushed them. The most terrifying moment was when I realized that this situation was inescapable, fated. In a couple of hours the building was occupied, men had been killed, and the troops turned and started moving toward the Parliament. It was clear to us that once the troops arrived at the Parliament building, the number of victims and wounded would multiply. Few of us expected what happened next—the troops would simply pass us by.

While Gorbachev's role in the Baltic events was unclear, it was evident that the Soviet state was willing to use its might against its own citizens to enforce central authority. The people, however, as a result of Gorbachev's reforms, were no longer willing to remain quiet. In Moscow, thousands took to the streets to protest the crackdown. On February 9, Lithuania voted for independence, and on March 3,

Latvia and Estonia followed. For the time being, the Kremlin watched the events disapprovingly.

The Fate of the Soviet Union

As the Baltic republics were breaking away from the union, the decision on the fate of the country was given to the people. Because Gorbachev was struggling to preserve the union while at the same time allowing the republics more autonomy, he decided to allow the people to make the decision. The proposal for the Union Treaty was put to a "referendum" vote—all citizens of the Soviet Union could vote either for or against preserving the union. While Yeltsin and several republics boycotted the vote, the referendum passed. In Russia, 71 percent of citizens voted in favor of preserving the Soviet Union.

But the outcome of the referendum in the Russian republic was not clear-cut. This was because Yeltsin had included an additional question in the Russian version of the vote that asked voters if they supported the idea of creating a new office of president of Russia. Seventy percent of Russians voted in favor of this proposal as well. The results were confusing. Russians had voted to preserve the union but had also voted to have their own president. Both Gorbachev and Yeltsin claimed victory.

In the following months, plans for both a new president of Russia and for a new union were underway. In June 1991,

Russians went to the polls and elected Yeltsin as the first president of Russia. Yeltsin was now the first democratically elected leader in Russian history. He began his work, using his new political power to secure added rights for the Russian republic while working with Gorbachev on a new union treaty. He negotiated the specifics of the new treaty, demanding that authority over taxes and the police, for example, be given to the republics. The new treaty was a victory for both Yeltsin and Gorbachev as the republics had significantly increased powers while the Soviet government maintained a central role. Gorbachev, Yeltsin, and Nursultan Nazarbayev, the leader of the Republic of Kazakhstan, planned to meet in August to sign the new treaty. Gorbachev hoped that other republics would sign after that.

The August Coup

The treaty not only gave the republics greater powers, but it also called for the Soviet president to be democratically elected. This greatly endangered the conservatives who knew that any form of Soviet authoritarianism would no longer be tolerated. Several conservatives, therefore, planned to stage a coup to push Gorbachev out of office and take control of the government. Many of the men involved in the coup had been urging Gorbachev for many months to impose emergency rule in the country but he had refused. All were strongly opposed to the second

Boris Yeltsin

Boris Yeltsin was born on February 1, 1931, in Sverdlovsk, now Yekaterinburg. Yeltsin worked on various construction projects in his youth and joined the Communist Party when he was thirty. In 1976, he became the first chairman of the Sverdlovsk party committee, and in that role he met Mikhail Gorbachev. In 1985, Gorbachev promoted Yeltsin to head the Moscow Communist Party organization. The following year, Yeltsin was appointed to the Politburo. In 1987, after criticizing party leaders for moving too slowly on reform, he was let go from his Communist Party positions.

Yeltsin began his political comeback in 1989 when he ran for and was elected to the newly created Congress of People's Deputies of the Soviet Union. In 1990, Yeltsin was also elected to another new parliament, this one at the Russian republic level. Only months later, he renounced the Communist Party completely, stunning Gorbachev and other leaders. In June 1991, Yeltsin was elected to the new post of president of Russia in historic republic-wide elections. Yeltsin had become Russia's first popularly elected leader in all of its history. During the August 1991 coup against Gorbachev, Yeltsin was spurred into action. While Gorbachev was detained in his summer home, Yeltsin led the resistance, rallying supporters in Moscow against the coup plotters. His defiance against the coup plotters made him an instant hero to the Russian people.

After the fall of the Soviet Union, Yeltsin continued as the president of Russia until December 31, 1999. His presidency was filled with ups and downs, significant victories, and shattering setbacks. One setback was Yeltsin's health. He underwent major heart surgery in 1996; this and other problems continued to plague him throughout the remainder of his administration. As his own health, Russia's economy, and the war in Chechnya deteriorated simultaneously, Yeltsin seemed less and less able to run the country. Once Russia's hero, Yeltsin grew increasingly unpopular. On New Year's Eve 1999, Yeltsin surprised the world by announcing his resignation. This gave then-prime minister Vladimir Putin the title of acting president for several months. Putin won the Russian presidency in the spring of 2000.

Bush (left) and Yeltsin meet at Camp David.

union treaty. Their timing was a desperate attempt to defeat the signing of the treaty.

Just before the planned signing of the treaty, on August 19, 1991, in an exciting, dangerous, and illegal move, several high-level officials made an attempt to take governmental control from Gorbachev. Gorbachev was away from the capital on vacation at a summer home at Foros on the Crimean Peninsula on the Black Sea. Eight old-guard communists decided to make their move. Broadcast over Soviet radio and television, the men declared themselves the State Committee for the State of Emergency. They told the country that Gorbachev was too ill to perform his duties. The committee declared a state of emergency, banned protests and strikes, announced a curfew, and restricted the media. Conservative vice president Gennadi Yanayev assumed the presidency. Meanwhile, in Foros, Gorbachev was placed under house arrest and his telephones and other means of communication were cut off. It seemed that reform and democracy had come to a quick end.

But the State Committee did not restrict or arrest Yeltsin. Despite the tensions between the rising Russian republic and the central Soviet government, Yeltsin came forward to support Gorbachev as the legitimate Soviet leader. While the coup plotters gathered inside the Kremlin, Yeltsin came outside to communicate with the people. Speaking in front of the White House, the building that houses the Russian government,

Yeltsin denounced the coup and its plotters and demanded Gorbachev's release. His words were read over independent radio and sent through Western wire services. Despite the blocks on Soviet media, he was heard throughout the vast Soviet Union. In this courageous speech, Yeltsin said,

> Undoubtedly it is essential to give the country's president, Gorbachev, an opportunity to address the people. Today he has been blockaded. I have been denied communications with him. . . . We are absolutely confident that our countrymen will not permit the sanctioning of the tyranny and lawlessness of the putschists [plotters], who have lost all shame and conscience. We address an appeal to servicemen to manifest lofty civic duty and not take part in the reactionary coup. Until these demands are met, we appeal for a universal unlimited strike.[60]

Yeltsin had quickly emerged as the leader of the opposition to the coup. He summoned thirty tanks to stand guard around the White House. At one point Yeltsin even jumped on a tank to address the crowd. With his fist raised in the air, he symbolized the strength and will of the people to oppose this illegal act. Supporters flooded the streets around him and throughout Moscow. In other Russian cities as well, local leaders and citizens were motivated to action. In Leningrad, for example,

over two hundred thousand people rushed to show support for Mayor Anatoly Sobchak, who backed Yeltsin in the opposition to the coup.

People in faraway republics also rallied against the coup and showed their support of Gorbachev as the legitimate leader. Leaders of Kazakhstan, Kyrgyzstan, Lithuania, Latvia, Estonia, and Moldova actively denounced the coup. Many local Russian mayors announced their opposition as did Patriarch Aleksei, the head of the Russian Orthodox Church. Even leaders of the communist elite, the Soviet military and the KGB, refused to cooperate with the Emergency Committee.

Calling for resistance against the Soviet coup, Yeltsin (at left) speaks from the top of a tank in front of the White House.

The Final Defeat Means Victory for Yeltsin

The situation proved very dangerous as the coup plotters were not afraid, at least initially, to use force. On the night of August 20, they ordered several armored personnel carriers to move toward the White House, where the carriers fatally crushed three young men who were faithful to Yeltsin. But Yeltsin and his supporters stood firm, and in the end, the Emergency Committee was not willing to provoke more bloodshed. According to KGB chairman Vladimir Kruichkov, one of the members of the Emergency Committee, "We were not bloodthirsty. We were not ready to pay any price to hold onto power."[61] At 3 A.M., Kruichkov phoned Yeltsin and admitted defeat. Yeltsin sent a plane to bring Gorbachev back to Moscow.

Gorbachev at first did not understand the magnitude of what had happened and the swell of support surrounding Yeltsin. Returning to the capital, he condemned

America Reports on the August Coup in Moscow

On August 19, 1991, Americans awoke only to find out from their local papers that while they were sleeping an emergency coup had taken place in the Soviet Union. The *Washington Post* reported the events in the following abridged article by Michael Dobbs.

Close Aides Oust Gorbachev, Hard-Line Group Takes Over, Committee Declares State of Emergency To Save Soviet Union

AUG. 19 (MONDAY)—A group of President Mikhail Gorbachev's close aides today announced that it had taken over power and established a state of emergency in order to save the Soviet Union from ethnic disintegration and economic chaos. Early morning broadcasts on television and radio named Vice President Gennady Yanayev, 54, as head of a new "State Committee for the State of Emergency." The committee, which includes Prime Minister Valentin Pavlov, Defense Minister Dmitri Yasov and KGB chief Vladimir Kryuchkov, said it was assuming all power in the country because of Gorbachev's "inability to perform his duties for health reasons." Gorbachev, 60, has been vacationing on the Black Sea coast, and there was no immediate word of his whereabouts.

Independent Soviet journalists said that columns of tanks and armored cars had been observed in several parts of Moscow, particularly around sensitive communications facilities. The radio and television center at Ostankino, in the north of the city, has been surrounded by armed troops and nobody was allowed into the building, the journalists said.

The seizure of power by the group of conservative politicians came on the eve of the signing of a new treaty of union that would have reshaped the country as a loosely bound confederation of sovereign states. The treaty also would have resulted in the dissolution of the existing all-union power structures and the holding of fresh elections.

A decree signed by Yanayev said that a state of emergency had been imposed on "some parts of the Soviet Union" for a period of six months in order to restore peace and establish the supremacy of all-union legislation. The proclamation described the emergency measures as "temporary," saying that they were not intended to interrupt the process of "profound reforms." Yanayev said in the statement that he was taking over the president's duties under Article 127 of the Soviet constitution. It allows the vice president to assume power in the event the president is unable to perform his duty.

In an address to the nation, the committee said that the political and economic reform movement launched six years ago by Gorbachev "had gone into a blind alley" and a "mortal danger" hangs over the country. It said that the destabilization of the political and economic situation in the Soviet Union was undercutting the country's position as a world power.

the coup plotters saying, "These people took advantage of the difficulties of the transitional period, and the tension in society and anxiety about what is going to happen to us, and decided to carry out far-fetched plans that would have plunged our society into utter turmoil."[62] He also noted that things had changed irreversibly. "I have come back . . . to another country, and I myself am a different man now."[63]

Yeltsin, showing his resolve and political adeptness to stop the coup, had clearly won the political spotlight. His leadership and courage throughout the event had motivated the people to oppose the coup. The figure of Yeltsin standing on the tank with his fist raised in the air was a moment of great pride for Russians and the Russian republic. He masterminded plans to outwit the coup plotters and used new technologies to communicate with the West despite the fact that the regular phone lines had been disconnected. In addition, he caused a state of confusion among the plotters themselves by leaking unconfirmed internal reports that some of them had resigned. According to Yeltsin biographer John Morrison, "Yeltsin's conduct during the coup displayed more than just courage; he not only outfaced but outsmarted the coup leaders, with a mixture of bluff and cunning."[64]

Although the opposition to the coup had been based on the notion that Gorbachev was the legitimate leader of the country, things were no longer the same in the country. Gorbachev had been over- shadowed by Yeltsin. Before Gorbachev could get his footing in the new climate in Moscow, Yeltsin quickly took over several Soviet departments and powers, such as the military, and reassigned them to the Russian government. On August 23, Yeltsin even banned the activities of the Communist Party of the Soviet Union and suspended the publication of the main party newspaper *Pravda* and other state-run newspapers. His leadership encouraged other republics to follow his lead. Leaders of other republics soon banned or suspended their republic's Communist Party.

The End of the Soviet Union

Ultimately, the coup had destroyed the credibility of communism, the central government, Gorbachev himself, and the Soviet Union. On August 24, Gorbachev resigned as the leader of the Soviet Communist Party. Only a few days later, the party itself dissolved. Although Gorbachev, still the Soviet president, continued to try to work out a future for the Soviet Union, he had lost all political standing. In December, Yeltsin met with Leonid Kravchuk from Ukraine and Stanislav Shushkevich from Belarus to discuss the future of the union. They had not even bothered to invite Gorbachev to the meeting. Together, the three leaders signed a pact that announced the end of the Soviet Union and the creation of the Commonwealth of Independent States in its place. One week later, accepting what had essentially already been decided

Young children sit on a toppled statue of Joseph Stalin. In 1991 the Soviet Union was dissolved and replaced by fifteen independent states.

without him, Gorbachev announced that the Soviet central government would cease to exist by the end of the year.

Although the precise end of the Cold War is heavily debated, the end of the Soviet Union was certainly a defining event. The crystallizing moment for Americans came on Christmas Day, 1991, when Gorbachev called President George H.W. Bush to wish him a Merry Christmas and to tell him that it was his last day in office. Later, in President Bush's Christmas broadcast to the nation, he spoke of the struggle against communism and the end of the Cold War. "For over 40 years the United States led the West in the struggle against communism and the threat it posed to our most precious values. This struggle shaped the lives of all Americans.

It forced all nations to live under the specter of nuclear destruction. That confrontation is now over."[65] That night, in Moscow the flag of the Soviet Union, with its red background and gold hammer and sickle, flew for the last time over the Kremlin. Although he had never planned to abandon the ideals of socialism and had fervently resisted the break up of the Soviet Union, Gorbachev spoke respectfully in January 1992 when he said, "I do not regard the end of the Cold War as a victory for one side. . . . The end of the Cold War is our common victory."[66]

The United States and Russia Are New Allies

More than ten years have passed since the end of the Cold War. Throughout these ten years, both the United States and Russia have worked to find their new roles in the world. Russia and the other fourteen independent countries formed from the breakup of the Soviet Union have faced great challenges, including building new governments and political systems and dealing with the economic decay inherited from decades of communism. For Russia, the path toward a more democratic society has not been easy. And despite the fact that Russia and the United States now share more similar views, the relationship and cooperation between them in the past ten years has also been challenging and somewhat complicated.

As Russia emerged from the ruins that were once the Soviet Union, many U.S. policy makers and other Americans believed that the country would quickly transition to a democracy and market economy. Having completed this process, Russia would be a close and cooperative partner in world events. But Russia's transition in the 1990s did not progress as resolutely as the United States had hoped, and this fact continued to make the U.S.- Russian relationship a tricky and evolving affair.

A Rocky Relationship

At first it seemed as if a strategic and friendly partnership would blossom. America's new president, Bill Clinton, elected in 1992, and Russian president Boris Yeltsin got along well. Their first official summit took place in Vancouver, Canada, in May 1993. The summit was a precursor of things to come. Yeltsin's behavior proved erratic: He often tried to goad or wheedle Clinton into certain agreements, and in the evenings he generally drank generous amounts of alcohol and grew rowdy. But Clinton did not seem to mind. He understood that the Russian leader, like his country, was full of contradictions. During this first summit, Clinton demonstrated his easy-going approach to Russia, telling his communications director George Stephanopoulos to report to the media that he had found Yeltsin full of "vinegar, a real fighter."[67] Revealing that he understood both Russia and its leader were facing real challenges, he added, "I do my best when I'm under the gun, and so does this guy. He's not deterred by long odds, and now he's at the top of his form."[68]

Yeltsin had come to the summit as the president of a country that was undergoing a radical transformation from a communist system to one based on democratic principles and market economics. This transition was sure to be a difficult one. Despite Yeltsin's high approval rating among Russian citizens, Russia's legislature was still dominated by conservative communists who were determined to impeach the president. In this atmosphere, America could help Russia. Clinton offered Yeltsin aid for the transition process, but the Russian president voiced concern that while the country needed support, he was wary of accepting too much help from America. He worried that communist conservatives at home would criticize his actions if he allowed Russia to come "under the U.S.'s thumb."[69]

Perhaps this was the reason for the restrained response from the U.S. government during Russia's post-Soviet period. The transformation from a communist

Yeltsin and U.S. president Bill Clinton discuss politics in a peaceful setting at the Vancouver summit.

system to a democratic one, especially for a large country such as Russia, would undoubtedly affect every aspect of society. Yet despite the massive changes that were needed to completely reinvent the system, Western aid was insignificant. This was evident even in the immediate months after the Soviet collapse, when then-president George H. W. Bush did not render large amounts of aid that would help to rebuild the country in the post–Cold War era.

In fact, rather than engaging Russia in an international dialogue and supporting real reform at an early stage, one of the first steps taken by the Western community was to demand that Russia pay back the Soviet debt. Although it did not have any debt of its own, Russia took on the debt accrued by the Soviet Union in exchange for Soviet foreign assets (property such as the former Soviet embassies in other countries). International institutions demanded that Russia quickly pay its massive and crippling financial obligations. This was not a supportive policy for a fledgling new country.

Much of the difficulties in the U.S.-Russian relationship encountered in the 1990s can be traced back to unrealistic expectations. The U.S. government first hoped that Russia would quickly implement political and economic systems similar to or even modeled after the democratic and market-oriented system found in the United States. But after hundreds of years of czarist rule and seventy years of communist rule, reform of the system would not come easily. At the same time, given the country's unique history, Russia probably did not plan to model its system after that of the United States. Instead, Russia sought to find a political and economic system that worked best for its people and its history.

Nonetheless, Russia changed dramatically during the 1990s. While Yeltsin was sometimes seen as having autocratic tendencies, at least with regards to holding on to the presidency as long as possible, the political system became more democratic in many respects. Free and fair elections now take place at all levels of government. In addition, the economy was moving from a centrally planned to a market-oriented one. Most state assets were privatized, meaning that things such as apartments, stores, restaurants, companies, and factories, all previously owned by the government, were now sold or transferred to individual or private-company ownership. In addition, the government freed prices and expanded trade opportunities with foreign countries. Formerly closed off to the outside world, citizens can travel freely both within and outside the country. Western products, such as Mercedes cars, French perfume, and American jeans are now abundantly available in Russia. Russia's people are open to and interested in the world, and Russia has become an integrated part of the international community.

However, many U.S. policy makers have criticized Russia during its transition period. Many Americans believe that the pace and scope of change in Russia has been too slow and limited. Russia's continued corruption, growing mafia, and lack of law enforcement has made investment and trade relations difficult. In addition, troubles in Chechnya, a republic located in Russia, have also led to strained relations.

Unwelcome Criticism: Chechnya

Shortly after the breakup of the Soviet Union, the republic of Chechnya became a problem for Moscow when it declared independence from Russia. Chechnya, a Muslim republic in the southern part of the country, announced that it would rule over its own affairs. Moscow, however, was unwilling to allow the republic to secede. Many of the people living in Chechnya, it appeared, also did not want to leave Russia. Moscow supported their stance and sent tanks into the city of Grozny in 1994. Bloody fighting resulted in thousands of deaths, the complete destruction of the city, and Russia's eventual and upsetting retreat.

The situation in Chechnya, however, was not easily solved. Tensions between Russian and Chechen leaders continued to flare throughout the next few years. Fighting between Russian troops and Chechen rebels first reignited in 1996. The situation was quickly settled when both sides signed a treaty allowing the re-

gion greater autonomy, but in 1999 tensions flared again. Chechen guerrillas attacked people in the neighboring Russian republic of Dagestan. Russian officials grew angry and began an operation to wipe out the Chechen guerrillas. This operation continues to this day.

Although it has done little to interfere in the matter, America has continually and severely criticized Russia's actions in Chechnya. The American media has focused on the number of civilians killed in Chechnya. In addition, Western reports have focused on the brute force and unorthodox practices employed by Russian troops in Chechnya on several occasions, a fact that is severely condemned by the United States. While defending its actions as part of a domestic Russian problem, Moscow has not taken America's criticism lightly. The Chechen situation has represented one of the most notable and ongoing disagreements between the United States and Russia.

War in Yugoslavia

Another low point in U.S.-Russian relations came when the United States and the North Atlantic Treaty Organization (NATO; the alliance of Western countries originally created in 1949 to defend Europe against communism, has now expanded membership and outlook to support European security) decided to intervene in the war in Yugoslavia, where ethnic republics within the Yugoslav federation declared their independence

The Russian Mafia

Since 1991, the growing mafia has been one of Russia's greatest problems. Organized crime, or Russian mafia groups, originated in the late Soviet era when the state loosened its control over the economy and corruption gained momentum. When Russia became an independent country, Russian organized crime took advantage of the volatile and changing situation and expanded its illegal activities. By the mid-1990s, there were more than five thousand different organized criminal groups throughout Russia.

Gaining strength and membership, Russian organized crime groups came to control many aspects of the Russian economy, for example, by bribing police officers to ignore their illegal acts while they extort payments from everyday business owners. In other criminal acts, government officials and foreigners have been the targets of shootouts, many of which took place in Moscow in broad daylight.

The Russian mafia has certainly hindered democracy and a normal market economy in Russia. It has also had implications for the post–Cold War relationship between the United States and Russia. In 1999, for example, a huge illegal money-laundering scheme was uncovered at the Bank of New York, and federal officials were quick to point to the involvement of the Russian mafia. It was alleged that billions of dollars from Russia, much of it from mafia groups, had been channeled through U.S. accounts. Although the allegations were not proven, at the time the press was highly critical of both the Clinton administration and the Yeltsin government. Such scandals continue. In 2002, a reputed Russian crime boss was arrested in Italy for allegedly fixing two figure skating events at the Salt Lake City Olympics. During the Olympics, the Russian press highly criticized the proceedings as being rigged by Americans. Such examples are evidence of the continued rivalry between the two nations.

A greater danger of organized crime relates to the fact that Russia still has large amounts of poorly guarded weapons of mass destruction and radioactive materials. The possibility that Russian criminals might obtain these materials or weapons and then sell them to terrorists is of grave concern to the United States and other countries.

from the central government. The situation was further confounded by a number of different ethnic groups that had clashed throughout history in their cultures and beliefs. In the mid-1990s, the situation quickly escalated into a bloody civil war. While Western countries supported the rights of the ethnic republics, Russia defended the position of the Yugoslav central government. Feeling a close bond with the Serbs, a Slavic people with Orthodox Christian beliefs similar to those of Russians, many Russian volunteers went to Yugoslavia to fight alongside fellow Serbs. At the same time, Western countries that condemned the position of the Yugoslav government decided to intervene.

NATO bombed Sarajevo in the fall of 1995. This led to extreme anger in Moscow. When Yeltsin came to New York to speak at the UN General Assembly in October 1995, he severely criticized NATO's bombing campaign. He warned that any further actions pointed to even worsening relations, or a "new era of confrontation."[70]

NATO bombed Yugoslavia again in 1999, which caused a further worsening of U.S.-Russian relations. Relations were at an all-time low as many spoke of a new cold war or worse. NATO bombed Belgrade again in 1999, injuring relations further.

The issue of NATO enlargement was another thorny topic for superpower relations. During the Soviet era, NATO had been used to defend Europe against communism. The Soviets countered the organization by establishing their own military alliance of East European countries called the Warsaw Pact. With the collapse of communism throughout Eastern Europe in 1989, the Warsaw Pact also dissolved. But NATO remained and began expanding its membership by accepting several former

Warsaw Pact countries such as the Czech republic, Poland, and Hungary as members. Russia received a limited voice in NATO affairs but has not been invited to join as a full member.

Despite the difficulties, the United States and Russia continued to make some progress in their relationship. During the Clinton and Yeltsin years, new agreements were made on arms reduction. Such successes were the product of the friendship forged between Yeltsin and Clinton. Even in the immediate aftermath of the NATO bombing campaign in

A group of Russian soldiers load shells in a cannon during a military campaign in Chechnya in 1996.

Bosnia, Yeltsin spoke of partnership to Clinton at a 1995 summit meeting in Hyde Park, New York. He said,

A Yugoslavian police barracks lies in ruins after a NATO bombing raid.

Bill, I want to say that our partnership remains strong and reliable. Even on tough problems, like Bosnia, we'll find solutions. Our partnership is the most valuable thing to us. Not only do we need it, but the whole world needs it. You and I might leave the scene, but what we have accomplished together will survive as our legacy. This is the main theme that we must develop between us. It's you and me, Bill and Boris.[71]

A New Century and New Leaders

In 2000, new presidents came into power in both Russia and the United States and this meant a new direction for U.S.-Russian relations. In Russia, Yeltsin stepped down and fresh elections brought Vladimir Putin, a city official from St. Petersburg, into the Russian presidency. In the United States, George W. Bush, the son of former president George H. W. Bush and the former governor of Texas, entered the White House in January 2001.

At first it seemed that relations would be on a path of decline. Because Putin was a former KGB professional, the United States expressed concern about the future of Russia's democracy. And because President Bush did not initially seem concerned with engaging Russia in a new dialogue, it seemed that any real constructive partnership between the two countries was unlikely. But interestingly, Bush and Putin have found a common dialogue. Both men are pragmatists and sportsmen, and the two leaders seem to get along well. After meeting Putin for the first time, in fact, President Bush spoke of their strong chemistry. He said he had "looked the man in the eye," and "was able to get a sense of his soul."[72]

Putin has been both praised and criticized in the West, making the new U.S.-Russian relationship difficult to pinpoint. While Putin has employed some anti-democratic measures, such as centralizing his power and putting restrictions on the media, he has been praised for his commitment to economic reform. Immediately after coming into office, Putin put together a strong team of economic advisors who boasted immediate accomplishments including tax reform and a balanced budget. While focusing on solving Russia's domestic problems—first and foremost the economy—Putin understands that strong relations with the West can only help Russia in achieving this task.

Cooperation After September 11, 2001

The terrorist attacks on the United States on September 11, 2001, were a major turning point in U.S.-Russian relations. After this terrifying assault, in which nearly three thousand people died when terrorists hijacked planes that crashed into the two towers of the World Trade Center in Manhattan, into the Pentagon near Washington, D.C., and into a field near Shanksville, Pennsylvania, many world leaders expressed support for the United States. Putin, in fact, was the first foreign leader to contact President Bush after the attack to express his condolences. Russia also quickly rendered assistance to the United States and the international coalition fighting in Afghanistan. Russia shared its military intelligence, supplied arms to the Northern Alliance (the group fighting against the terrorist forces who are believed to have been behind the attacks), and did not object to the United States using military bases in the neighboring countries of Kyrgyzstan, Tajikistan, and Uzbekistan. These were significant contributions and were not overlooked by American policy makers.

Prior to September 11, the United States could not have imagined that Russia would accept U.S. military presence in Central Asia or that Russia would share its classified military intelligence. But Putin quickly positioned Russia as one of the United States' most important allies in the international war against terrorism.

The United States Withdraws from ABM Arms Control Treaty

In December 2001 the United States announced that it was withdrawing from the Antiballistic Missile (ABM) Treaty with Russia. The ABM Treaty, signed in 1972 by U.S. president Richard Nixon and Soviet general secretary Leonid Brezhnev, was part of an important framework of agreements that set limits on weapons of mass destruction and their testing. This arms control agreement helped to give the world a greater sense of stability during the height of the Cold War.

The administration of George W. Bush decided to withdraw from the treaty because of new and emerging threats to American national security. The terrorist attacks on September 11, 2001, demonstrated that the United States has new enemies since the end of the Cold War. Countries and groups in the Middle East, South Asia, and other places possess weapons of mass destruction, while other groups are actively seeking such weapons. The Bush administration decided that these entities pose a direct threat to U.S. security. Bush argued that the United States needs to have the flexibility to develop, test, and deploy antiballistic missile systems for defensive purposes. Speaking of the necessity to defend against terrorists on December 13, 2001, President Bush announced, "I have concluded the ABM treaty hinders our government's ability to develop ways to protect our people from future terrorist . . . attacks." He later

added that "[d]efending the American people is my highest priority as commander in chief and I cannot and will not allow the United States to remain in a treaty that prevents us from developing effective defenses." Bush's remarks can be found in full on the Federation of American Scientists website at www.fas.org.

The U.S. withdrawal from the ABM Treaty was heavily disapproved of in Moscow. President Vladimir Putin said that while the American decision was not unexpected, he believed it was made in error. He said that the ABM Treaty represented the mutual cooperation between the United States and Russia. But despite his strong disapproval of the move, Putin's reaction was muted. In remarks aired by the British Broadcasting Corporation, he emphasized that the decision would not have a strong impact on U.S.-Russian relations, and it would "not pose a threat to the national security of the Russian Federation." In Russia, many citizens are not as certain. Many feel that Putin has given up too much to the United States, sharing important intelligence information with Washington after September 11, 2001, for example, while receiving very little from the United States in return. For many Russians, America's withdrawal from the ABM Treaty represents what they perceive to be a pattern: The U.S. government pushes forth its agenda for its own purposes with little to offer its post–Cold War partner, Russia.

In contrast to the Cold War period, Russia now seems to view the United States not as a threat but as a partner. Solidarity was evident between the two countries when, on September 13, flags flew at half-mast throughout Russia.

The terrorist attacks on September 11 also strengthened the U.S.-Russian relationship as it changed the American per-

spective on Chechnya. The Kremlin had long asserted that Osama bin Laden, the prime suspect in the terrorist attacks on the United States, funded and trained rebels in Chechnya. Moscow blamed Chechen and international terrorists for bombings that occurred in Moscow and in other Russian cities in 1999 that claimed hundreds of lives. The Bush administration radically reversed its earlier position and now shows new sympathy for the Russian aims in Chechnya. For the first time, the United States has acknowledged the presence of international Islamic threats and possible international terrorist support to Chechen rebels. Previously, this notion was ignored or downplayed in the U.S. government. This new outlook is another example of an evolving partnership.

The north tower of the World Trade Center crumbles after terrorists fly a commercial airliner into the building on September 11, 2001.

The 2002 Putin-Bush Summit

In support of this partnership, Russia hosted President Bush for a summit meeting in Moscow and St. Petersburg, Russia, in May 2002. The focus of the summit was an arms reduction treaty that limited nuclear warheads in both countries to between seventeen hundred and twenty-two hundred by 2012. The treaty also stipulated that a portion of the warheads be destroyed and another portion be stored. This point was a major concession for Putin who advocated the destruction of all launchers in part because storage is a costly and difficult endeavor.

The signing of the Strategic Offensive Reductions Treaty showed the world that Russia is still an important world player. The American and Russian presidents signed a treaty that, in essence, demonstrates they are partners in the world. Despite the fact that he made concessions in the treaty, Putin believed that signing such a treaty with the United States proves that Russia, like the United States, is still a major superpower. Putin hopes to demonstrate that Russia is a major

Why Russia Still Matters to the United States

In *Russia's Decline and Uncertain Recovery*, Thomas E. Graham Jr. gives eight reasons why good relations with Russia remain important to the United States even after more than ten years since the end of the Cold War:

> First, Russia's geographical position places it abreast of regions of strategic interest to the United States: Europe, East and South Asia, and the Persian Gulf. The future . . . balances in these regions will depend on what happens to Russia. . . .

> Second, despite its strategic weakness, Russia remains the dominant power vis-à-vis the countries of the former Soviet Union, which are . . . weaker and more fragile states. Russia has—and for years to come will continue to have—a tremendous capacity to intervene in the affairs of these states, for both good and evil. . . .

> Third, Russia remains by far the richest country in the world in natural resources, including many strategic metals of which it is the sole or major supplier. [These resources] ensure that Russia's landmass will remain critical to the world's economy. . . .

> Fourth, Russia retains a veto in the U.N. Security Council, and barring an unlikely radical reorganization of that body, it will continue to do so well into the future. . . .

> Fifth, because Russia harbors a large nuclear arsenal, extensive facilities for building, storing, and experimenting with weapons of mass destruction, and thousands of scientists and engineers with the know-how to build such weapons, it will remain a source of significant concern. . . .

> Sixth, with its large nuclear arsenal, Russia remains the only country in the world with the ability to destroy the United States. Although it is highly improbable that Russia's leaders would ever launch a suicidal attack . . . the danger of accidents remains. . . .

> Seventh, the United States' ability to deepen its ties with its key allies, particularly in Europe, will depend to some degree on its skill in managing relations with Russia.

> Eighth, it should never be forgotten that Russia could rebuild—and with greater success and at a faster rate than anyone anticipates.

decision maker in world politics and a solid partner of the West. According to the *Economist*, "After 70 years of blind-alley communism, and ten more of drift, Mr. Putin is making a determined bid for Russia to end its self-estrangement and join the concert [group] of developed, democratic countries alongside America and Europe."[73]

The United States has verified that the treaty, to be concluded at the St. Petersburg summit, is a sign of real partnership. After announcing the treaty, President Bush said that the agreement proved that the Cold War was over. He stated that the treaty would "liquidate the legacy of the cold war."[74] The cooperative and constructive relationship between the two countries is especially amazing given the many years of distrust and dislike that dominated the Cold War. U.S. national security adviser Condoleeza Rice confirmed this idea, stating, "To see the kind of relationship that presidents Bush and Putin have developed and to see Russia firmly anchored in the west, that's really a dream of 300 years, not just of the post–cold war era."[75]

NATO-Russia Council

Further proof that Russia has joined the West is found in its acceptance of and participation in an expanded NATO. In May 2002, a new NATO-Russia Council was created when foreign ministers from the nineteen NATO member countries and Russia met in Reykjavik, Iceland. The new council will set joint international policy on specific issues. These issues will include counterterrorism, proliferation of nuclear, chemical, and biological weapons, missile defense, and peacekeeping efforts. The NATO-Russia Council is historic because it gives Russia a real voice on a number of very important issues. Announcing the deal, NATO secretary general George Robertson said, "It is impossible to overstate the importance of this recognition that NATO and Russia must stand side by side in defense of common values and interests in the face of the challenges of the new century."[76] American policy makers agreed with this new role for Russia. U.S. secretary of state Colin Powell said, "A strong basis for a new partnership is being forged."[77] Other Western officials pointed to the fact that the council gave further proof that the Cold War is over. British foreign secretary

Jack Straw said, "The Cold War is finished. Done. Kaput."[78]

Common Ground

Despite the fact that many Americans now have a favorable view of Russia, unfortunately many Russians are more skeptical about the relationship. Many Russians believe that in exchange for its assistance in the war on terrorism, Russia deserves concessions from the United States. This could include a dialogue on restructuring its Soviet-era debt to the West, and more importantly, its entry into the World Trade Organization, an international organization that sets the rules of trade among member countries. Despite the friendly position of President Putin, many in Russia believe that the current situation is one-sided, with the United States at a great advantage. This situation has quietly stoked anti-U.S. feelings among a majority of Russians.

Despite some dissent among Russians, the U.S.-Russian diplomatic relationship is at an all-time high. Presidents Bush and Putin have found many issues that they can cooperate on that are in the interests of both countries. The two countries have found that they can work together on important world issues such as combating terrorism. In fact, once archenemies now look more like allies. Despite more than forty-five years of combating ideologies and a world competition to outdo one another, the United States and Russia now have similar goals.

Secretary of State Colin Powell (center) joins foreign ministers to inaugurate the new NATO-Russia Council at the 2002 NATO conference.

To some extent, the United States has accepted that Russia might not be a democracy that exactly mirrors its own. Russia, especially after September 11, has realized that it too has a great deal to contribute to the United States. Both countries have discovered that they can work together to promote peace and security in the world. President Putin, in a speech to the Russian embassy in November 2001, highlighted the new cooperation between Russia and the United States, stating,

> The fortunes of our nations are different. For many years they had been moving along different paths. But if we look back at more than two centuries of our relations, one thing would strike you: at dramatic turning points in history, in the moments of truth, when the very existence of our nations were at stake, Russia and the United States have always stood together. . . . I am sure now, when our destiny meets history again, we will be not only partners, but also friends.[79]

★ Notes ★

Introduction: A Dramatic End to an Uncertain Era

1. Quoted in www.cnn.com/specials/cold.war.
2. Quoted in www.cnn.com/specials/cold.war.

Chapter 1: Reagan and the Final Freeze

3. Quoted in White House Website, www.whitehouse.gov.
4. Quoted in Jeremy Isaacs and Taylor Downing, *Cold War: An Illustrated History, 1945–1991*. Boston: Little, Brown, 1998, p. 333.
5. Quoted in Isaacs and Downing, *Cold War*, p. 334.
6. Ronald Reagan, Address to the Nation on Defense and National Security, March 23, 1983. www.cnn.com.
7. Quoted in Martin Walker, *The Cold War: A History*. New York: Henry Holt, 1993, p. 268.
8. Quoted in Mary Beth Norton et al., *A People and a Nation: A History of the United States*. Boston: Houghton Mifflin, 1982, p. 919.
9. Ronald Reagan, "Remarks at the Annual Convention of the National Association of Evangicals," Orlando, FL, March 8, 1983 www.ronaldreagan.com.
10. Quoted in Michael Kort, *The Columbia Guide to the Cold War*. New York: Columbia University Press, 1998, p. 78.

11. Quoted in Isaacs and Downing, *Cold War*, p. 342.
12. Quoted in Walker, *The Cold War*, p. 276.
13. Quoted in Don Oberdorfer, *From the Cold War to a New Era: The United States and the Soviet Union, 1983–1991*. Baltimore: Johns Hopkins University Press, 1998, pp. 72–73.

Chapter 2: Gorbachev and Change in the Soviet Union

14. Quoted in Isaacs and Downing, *Cold War*, p. 356.
15. Quoted in Isaacs and Downing, *Cold War*, p. 351.
16. Quoted in Isaacs and Downing, *Cold War*, p. 356.
17. Quoted in Michael McFaul, *Russia's Unfinished Revolution: Political Change from Gorbachev to Putin*. Ithaca, NY: Cornell University Press, 2001, p. 42.
18. Quoted in Isaacs and Downing, *Cold War*, p. 355.
19. Quoted in McFaul, *Russia's Unfinished Revolution*, p. 43.
20. Mikhail Gorbachev, general secretary of the Communist Party of the Soviet Union, speech at the Sofia Political Consultative Committee Meeting, October 22, 1985. www.isn.ethz.ch.

21. Archie Brown, *The Gorbachev Factor.* Oxford: Oxford University Press, 1996, p. 221.

Chapter 3: U.S.–Soviet Summits Work Toward Arms Reduction

22. Quoted in Oberdorfer, *From the Cold War to a New Era*, p. 140.
23. Quoted in Isaacs and Downing, *Cold War*, p. 359.
24. Quoted in Oberdorfer, *From the Cold War to a New Era*, p. 147.
25. Quoted in Oberdorfer, *From the Cold War to a New Era*, p. 147.
26. Quoted in Oberdorfer, *From the Cold War to a New Era*, p. 153.
27. Quoted in Isaacs and Downing, *Cold War*, p. 366.
28. Quoted in Isaacs and Downing, *Cold War*, p. 367.
29. Quoted in Oberdorfer, *From the Cold War to a New Era*, p. 205.
30. Quoted in Isaacs and Downing, *Cold War*, p. 367.
31. Quoted in Isaacs and Downing, *Cold War*, p. 367.
32. Quoted in Oberdorfer, *From the Cold War to a New Era*, p. 261.
33. Quoted in Oberdorfer, *From the Cold War to a New Era*, pp. 261–62.
34. Quoted in Oberdorfer, *From the Cold War to a New Era*, p. 293.
35. Oberdorfer, *From the Cold War to a New Era*, p. 294.
36. Oberdorfer, *From the Cold War to a New Era*, p. 295.
37. Mikhail Gorbachev, Speech to the United Nations, December 7, 1988. www.cnn.com/specials/cold.war.

Chapter 4: Revolutions in Eastern Europe, 1989

38. Isaacs and Downing, *Cold War*, p. 376.
39. Quoted in Isaacs and Downing, *Cold War*, p. 382.
40. Quoted in Isaacs and Downing, *Cold War*, p. 387.
41. David Remnick, *Lenin's Tomb: The Last Days of the Soviet Empire.* New York: Random House, 1993, p. 240.
42. Quoted in Isaacs and Downing, *Cold War*, p. 387.
43. Quoted in Vladimir Tismaneanu, *Reinventing Politics: Eastern Europe from Stalin to Havel.* New York: Free Press, 1992, p. 219.
44. Quoted in Tismaneanu, *Reinventing Politics*, p. 222.
45. Quoted in Gail Stokes, *The Walls Came Tumbling Down: The Collapse of Communism in Eastern Europe.* New York: Oxford University Press, 1993, p. 160.
46. Tismaneanu, *Reinventing Politics*, p. 233.
47. Quoted in Tismaneanu, *Reinventing Politics*, p. 234.

Chapter 5: Challenges to Communism Within the Soviet Union

48. Quoted in Mike Bowker, *Russian Foreign Policy and the End of the Cold War.* Aldershot, UK: Dartmouth, 1997, pp. 22–23.
49. Walter Isaacson, "A Long, Mighty Struggle," *Time*, April 10, 1989, p. 51.
50. Quoted in Isaacson, "A Long, Mighty Struggle," p. 51.

51. Quoted in Isaacson, "A Long, Mighty Struggle," p. 51.
52. Quoted in John Hiden and Patrick Salmon, *The Baltic Nations and Europe: Estonia, Latvia, and Lithuania in the Twentieth Century*. London: Longman, 1991, p. 155.
53. Hedrick Smith, *New Russians*. New York: Random House, 1990, p. 366.
54. Quoted in Isaacs and Downing, *Cold War*, p. 401.

Chapter 6: The Struggle to Preserve the Soviet Union

55. Raymond L. Garthoff, *The Great Transition: American-Soviet Relations and the End of the Cold War*. Washington, DC: The Brookings Institution, 1994, p.429.
56. Isaacs and Downing, *Cold War*, p. 401.
57. Quoted in Isaacs and Downing, *Cold War*, p. 406.
58. Quoted in www.cnn.com/specials/cold.war.
59. Quoted in www.cnn.com/specials/cold.war.
60. Boris Yeltsin's address of August, 19, 1991. www.cnn.com.
61. Quoted in www.cnn.com/specials/cold.war.
62. Quoted in www.cnn.com/specials/cold.war.
63. Quoted in Isaacs and Downing, *Cold War*, p. 416.
64. John Morrison, *Boris Yeltsin: From Bolshevik to Democrat*. New York: Dutton, 1991, p. 284.
65. Quoted in www.cnn.com/specials/cold.war.
66. Quoted in Isaacs and Downing, *Cold War*, p. 417.

Chapter 7: The United States and Russia Are New Allies

67. Quoted in Strobe Talbott, "Boris and Bill: Two Superpowers, Two Super Egos," *Washington Post Magazine*, May 26, 2002.
68. Quoted in Talbott, "Boris and Bill."
69. Quoted in Talbott, "Boris and Bill."
70. Quoted in Talbott, "Boris and Bill."
71. Quoted in Talbott, "Boris and Bill."
72. Quoted in Judy Dempsey and Richard Wolfe, "In from the Cold," *Financial Times*, May 15, 2002.
73. "To Russia for Love," *The Economist*, May 18, 2002, p. 11.
74. Quoted in "A Farewell to Armaments," *The Economist*, May 18, 2002, p. 29.
75. Quoted in Julian Berger "Bush's Love of Pootie-Poot Putin," *Guardian*, May 20, 2002.
76. Quoted in Colleen Barry, "NATO Links Itself with Russia," *Washington Post*, May 15, 2002, p. A19.
77. Quoted in George Gedda, "Russian, U.S. Relations on a Roll," *Johnson's Russia List*, May 15, 2002.
78. Gedda, "Russian, U.S. Relations on a Roll."
79. Vladimir Putin, speech at the Russian embassy in Washington DC, November 13, 2001, as quoted by Federal News Service, Inc. Reprinted by the Embassy of the Russian Federation, www.russianembassy.org.

★ Chronology of Events ★

1980

November: Ronald Reagan is elected president of the United States.

1981

December: General Wojciech Jarulzelski announces martial law in Poland; Lech Walesa and other Solidarity leaders are imprisoned.

1982

November: Walesa is released from prison in Poland.

November: Soviet Communist Party general secretary Leonid Brezhnev dies and is succeeded by Yuri Andropov.

1983

March: Reagan calls the Soviet Union an "evil empire"; Reagan announces his support for the Strategic Defense Initiative.

October: Walesa wins the Nobel Peace Prize; the United States invades Grenada to overthrow its Marxist government.

1984

February: Andropov dies and is replaced by Konstantin Chernenko.

May: U.S. Congress bans further aid to contras in Nicaragua.

November: Reagan is reelected president of the United States.

1985

March: Chernenko dies and Mikhail Gorbachev is selected as the general secretary of the Communist Party of the Soviet Union.

November: Gorbachev and Reagan hold their first summit in Geneva, Switzerland.

1986

April: Chernobyl nuclear accident takes place.

October: Gorbachev and Reagan meet for a summit in Reykjavik, Iceland.

December: Gorbachev releases dissident Andrei Sakharov from exile in Gorky.

1987

December: Gorbachev and Reagan meet for a summit in Washington, D.C.; they sign the Intermediate Nuclear Forces Treaty which bans all intermediate-range missiles from Europe.

December: *Time* names Gorbachev "Man of the Year."

1988

February: Gorbachev announces that the Soviet Union will withdraw all forces from Afghanistan within a year.

May: Reagan and Gorbachev meet for another summit, this time in Moscow.

November: George H. W. Bush is elected president of the United States.

December: In a speech to the UN General Assembly, Gorbachev announces unilateral reductions in Soviet troops and tanks in Eastern Europe.

1989

February: Poland's government holds roundtable talks with Solidarity.

March: The Soviet Union holds the first partially free elections in its history to the newly established Congress of People's Deputies.

June: Solidarity is victorious in Poland's legislative elections.

June: Hundreds of thousands of people come out in Hungary to pay tribute to Imre Nagy who was executed for his role in the 1956 Hungarian revolution.

August: Demonstrations begin in Prague to protest the 1968 invasion of Czechoslovakia.

October: In East Germany, Erich Honecker is ousted and replaced by Egon Krenz.

November: East Germany opens the Berlin Wall.

November: Communist leader Todor Zhivkov resigns in Bulgaria.

November: Demonstrations continue in Prague, communist leader Milos Jakes resigns.

December: Bush and Gorbachev meet in Malta.

December: Romanian dictator Nicolae Ceauşescu and his wife flee; they are captured, tried, and put to death by a firing squad.

December: Vaclav Havel is elected president of Czechoslovakia; he becomes the country's first noncommunist president since 1948.

1990

March: Lithuania declares independence from the Soviet Union; Estonia follows.

March: The Congress of People's Deputies deletes Article 6 from the Soviet constitution, and communists thereby lose their monopoly on power.

March: Hungary's parliament dissolves; multi-party elections for new parliament are held.

May: Boris Yeltsin is chosen as the chairman of the Russian Supreme Soviet.

May: Latvia declares independence from the Soviet Union.

May–June: Bush and Gorbachev hold a summit in Washington, D.C.

October: East Germany dissolves, Germany reunites as the Federal Republic of Germany.

October: Gorbachev wins the Nobel Peace Prize.

December: Walesa is elected president of Poland.

December: Soviet foreign minister Eduard Shevardnadze resigns and warns of approaching dictatorship in the Soviet Union.

1991

January: Soviet forces seize buildings in capital cities of Lithuania and Latvia;

nineteen people are killed in the events.

June: Russian citizens go to the polls and elect Yeltsin, the first-ever president of Russia.

July: The Warsaw Pact disbands.

August: Soviet Communist Party hard-liners stage an unsuccessful coup against Gorbachev.

December: Yeltsin, Leonid Kravchuk, and Stanislav Shushkevich sign documents to create the Commonwealth of Independent States; Gorbachev resigns; the Soviet Union officially ceases to exist.

1992

November: Bill Clinton is elected president of the United States.

1994

December: Moscow sends tanks into Grozny, Chechnya.

1995

September: The North Atlantic Treaty Organization (NATO) bombs Sarajevo.

1999

December: Yeltsin resigns and names Vladimir Putin as the interim president.

2000

March: Putin is elected president of Russia.

November: George W. Bush is elected president of the United States.

2001

September: Terrorist attacks are made on the Pentagon and World Trade Center.

December: The United States announces withdrawal from the Anti-Ballistic Missile Treaty.

2002

May: Bush and Putin meet in Moscow and St. Petersburg.

May: NATO-Russia Council is formed.

☆ For Further Reading ☆

Michael G. Kort, *The Cold War.* Brookfield, CT: Millbrook, 1994. A comprehensive and well-organized survey for young readers of the Cold War from World War II to the collapse of communism in the 1990s.

———, *The Handbook of the Former Soviet Union.* Brookfield, CT: Millbrook, 1997. An excellent resource on the former Soviet Union and its fifteen successor states. Maps, flags, important events, and significant people for each country are included.

———, *Mikhail Gorbachev.* New York: Watts, 1990. This biography of the former Soviet leader begins at his birth in 1931, covers his rise through the Communist Party hierarchy, and concludes with the collapse of communism in Eastern Europe in 1989.

James A. Warren. *Cold War: The American Crusade Against World Communism, 1945–91.* New York: Lothrop, Lee, and Shepard, 1996. A comprehensive survey of the Cold War for young readers, this book chronicles the main events and personalities of the period.

Websites

CIA Website: At Cold War's End, *At Cold War's End: US Intelligence on the Soviet Union and Eastern Europe, 1989–1991* (www.cia.gov). This website provides U.S. intelligence materials and documents on the Soviet Union during the period 1989–1991.

CIA Worldfact Book (www.cia.gov). This website provides country profiles with current information on the country's geography, government, economy, military, and other topics.

Cold War International History Project Website at the Woodrow Wilson International Center for Scholars (http://cwihp.si.edu). This project's website contains new information and analysis from the history of the Cold War, including previously inaccessible Communist documents.

Official Website of the Embassy of the Russian Federation (www.russianembassy.org). Here you can find information on U.S.-Russia summits, texts of official Russian speeches, and news from Russia as well as other information on the country.

✫ Works Consulted ✫

Books

Timothy Garton Ash, *The Magic Lantern: The Revolution of '89 Witnessed in Warsaw, Budapest, Berlin and Prague.* New York: Vintage, 1999. A readable first-hand account of the events in Eastern Europe in 1989.

Michael R. Beschloss and Strobe Talbott, *At the Highest Levels: The Inside Story of the End of the Cold War.* Boston: Little, Brown, 1993. A behind-the-scenes history of the Cold War endgame, this book brings to life the private conversations and understandings between George H. W. Bush and Mikhail Gorbachev.

Mike Bowker, *Russian Foreign Policy and the End of the Cold War.* Aldershot, UK: Dartmouth, 1997. A look at a number of issues related to Soviet foreign policy and its influence on the end of the Cold War.

Archie Brown, *The Gorbachev Factor.* Oxford: Oxford University Press, 1996. This book covers Mikhail Gorbachev's contribution to the dramatic changes that took place within the Soviet Union in the second half of the 1980s and early 1990s.

Karen Dawisha and Bruce Parrott, *Russia and the New States of Eurasia: The Politics of Upheaval.* Cambridge, England: Cambridge University Press, 1994. This book studies the transformation of the former Soviet republics into independent states and focuses on the central role of Russia.

John Lewis Gaddis, *We Now Know: Rethinking Cold War History.* Oxford: Oxford University Press, 1997. Gaddis uses recently available documents to look back at the Cold War. He places most of the blame on the actions of the Soviet Union.

Raymond L. Garthoff, *The Great Transition: American-Soviet Relations and the End of the Cold War.* Washington, DC: The Brookings Institution, 1994. Covers diplomatic relations between the two superpowers from 1981 until the collapse of the Soviet Union in 1991.

Thomas E. Graham Jr., *Russia's Decline and Uncertain Recovery.* Washington, DC: Carnegie Endowment for International Peace, 2002. This book analyzes the emerging Russia and some of the difficulties the country has faced over the last ten years.

John Hiden and Patrick Salmon, *The Baltic Nations and Europe: Estonia, Latvia, and Lithuania in the Twentieth*

Century. London: Longman, 1991. A review of the Baltic nations' histories, the book ends with the period just prior to the collapse of the Soviet Union.

Jeremy Isaacs and Taylor Downing, *Cold War: An Illustrated History, 1945–1991*. Boston: Little, Brown, 1998. This is a comprehensive overview written as a companion to the CNN television series. The book is complete with pictures, first-hand accounts, and interesting sidebars.

Michael Kort, *The Columbia Guide to the Cold War*. New York: Columbia University Press, 1998. An invaluable reference on the Cold War itself, this guide gives an overview of the Cold War, an encyclopedia of Cold War topics and important figures, a chronology of events, and a thorough bibliography of resources on all topics concerning the Cold War. Some discussion is included on the end of the Cold War.

———, *The Soviet Colossus: History and Aftermath*, 5th ed. Armonk, NY: Sharpe, 2001. This book includes a chapter on events in Russia after the demise of the Soviet Union.

Ralph B. Levering, *The Cold War: A Post–Cold War History*. Arlington Heights, IL: Harlan Davidson, 1994. A historical overview of the Cold War from the publisher's American History Series.

Michael McFaul, *Russia's Unfinished Revolution: Political Change from Gorbachev to Putin*. Ithaca, NY: Cornell University Press, 2001. An in-depth, scholarly yet readable examination of politics within the Russian Federation.

John Morrison, *Boris Yeltsin: From Bolshevik to Democrat*. New York: Dutton, 1991. Written by a former Reuters Moscow bureau chief, this book examines Boris Yeltsin's political career up to 1991.

Mary Beth Norton, David M. Katzman, Paul D. Escott, Howard P. Chudacoff, Thomas G. Paterson, and William M. Tuttle, *A People and a Nation: A History of the United States*. Boston: Houghton Mifflin, 1982. An overview of American history.

Don Oberdorfer, *From the Cold War to a New Era: The United States and the Soviet Union, 1983–1991*. Baltimore: Johns Hopkins University Press, 1998. The author, a former diplomatic correspondent for the *Washington Post*, chronicles the ending of the Cold War. The book includes great detail of the political and personal history as it unfolds before the reader.

David Remnick, *Lenin's Tomb: The Last Days of the Soviet Empire*. New York: Random House, 1993. The former Moscow correspondent for the *Washington Post* provides a look at Soviet life, its people, and its leaders from 1986 to 1991.

Nicholas V. Riasanovsky, *A History of Russia*. New York: Oxford University Press, 1984. This book is the authoritative source on Russian history.

Werner Sikorski and Rainer Laabs, *Checkpoint Charlie and the Wall: A Divided People*

Rebel. Berlin: Ullstein Buchverlage, 2000. The authors provide stories and pictures from the Berlin Wall.

Hedrick Smith, *The New Russians*. New York: Random House, 1990. Based on hundreds of interviews, this book offers an interesting look at the explosive changes taking place during Mikhail Gorbachev's leadership.

Joseph Smith, *The Cold War: 1945–1991*, Second Edition. Oxford: Blackwell, 1998. An overview of the history of the Cold War.

Gail Stokes, *The Walls Came Tumbling Down: The Collapse of Communism in Eastern Europe*. New York: Oxford University Press, 1993. The author provides a clear analysis of the history and events that led up to the 1989 revolutions in Eastern Europe.

Vladimir Tismaneanu, *Reinventing Politics: Eastern Europe from Stalin to Havel*. New York: Free Press, 1992. A comparative analysis of the disintegration of communism in Eastern Europe.

Martin Walker, *The Cold War: A History*. New York: Henry Holt, 1993. A British journalist who worked as a correspondent for the *Manchester Guardian* in Moscow in the 1980s gives a comprehensive account of the Cold War.

Boris Yeltsin, *Against the Grain*. New York: Summit, 1990. Russia's first president tells his story.

——, *The Struggle for Russia*. New York: Random House, 1994. Russia's first president gives an inside account of Russia's journey toward democracy.

Vladislav Zubok and Constantine Pleshakov, *Inside the Kremlin's Cold War: From Stalin to Khrushchev*. Cambridge, MA: Harvard University Press, 1996. The authors, Russian historians, provide a first-of-its-kind, scholarly look at the Cold War using newly opened Soviet archives.

Periodicals

Colleen Barry, "NATO Links Itself with Russia," *Washington Post*, May 15, 2002, p. A19.

Julian Borger, "Bush's Love of Pootie-Poot Putin," *Guardian*, May 20, 2002.

Robert Cottrell, "Putin Policy Shift Is Bold But Risky," *Financial Times*, April 15, 2002.

Judy Dempsey and Richard Wolfe, "In from the Cold," *Financial Times*, May 15, 2002.

Michael Dobbs, "Close Aides Oust Gorbachev, Hard-Line Group Takes Over, Committee Declares State of Emergency to Save Soviet Union," *Washington Post*, August 19, 1991.

"A Farewell to Armaments," *Economist*, May 18, 2002.

George Gedda, "Russian, U.S. Relations on a Roll," *Johnson's Russia List*, May 15, 2002.

Paul Hofheinz, "Hot, Hot, Hot: Brigada S," *Time*, April 10, 1989.

"Holding Back," *Time*, April 10, 1989.

Walter Isaacson, "A Long, Mighty Struggle," *Time,* April 10, 1989.

Steven Mufson and Sharon LaFraniere, "ABM Withdrawal a Turning Point in Arms Control," *Washington Post,* December 13, 2001.

Strobe Talbott, "Boris and Bill: Two Superpowers, Two Super Egos," *Washington Post Magazine,* May 26, 2002.

"To Russia for Love," *Economist,* May 18, 2002.

"Vladimir Putin's Long, Hard Haul," *Economist,* May 18, 2002.

Websites

CNN Interactive Site on the Cold War (www.cnn.com). Created to complement the CNN Cold War documentary series, this site contains the documentary's script, as well as a knowledge bank, a debate and discussion area, articles and documents from the period, interviews, and an interactive game. This is one of the best resources for the Cold War.

Library of Congress (www.loc.gov). Revelations from the Russian Archives offer primary source materials from the Soviet Union with translations and explanations.

National Archives Records Administration (www.nara.gov). The U.S. National Archives Administration is the government's official record keeper. The website includes records of Congress and of presidential libraries.

National Security Archive (www.gwu.edu). The Archive is an independent, nongovernmental research institute and library that collects and disseminates declassified documents acquired through the Freedom of Information Act. The site includes online exhibits, interviews, and projects including "Openness in Russia and Eastern Europe."

Ronald Reagan Official Website (www.ronaldreagan.com). This site includes an in-depth look at various periods in Ronald Reagan's career and includes some of his best-known speeches.

The White House Website (www.whitehouse.gov). This is the official website for the current White House. It includes information on U.S. governmental policies, news, and major speeches.

Internet Sources

"America Withdraws from ABM Treaty," *BBC News,* December 13, 2001. http://news.bbc.co.uk.

Speech of Mikhail Gorbachev, general secretary of the Communist Party of the Soviet Union, at the Sofia Political Consultative Committee Meeting, October 22, 1985. www.isn.ethz.ch.

"Text: U.S. Diplomatic Notes on ABM Treaty," December 14, 2001. www.fas.org.

"Transcript: Bush Announces U.S. Withdrawal from ABM Treaty," December 13, 2001. www.fas.org.

"U.S. ABM Treaty Withdrawal Not Expected to Hurt Ties with Russia," December 14, 2001. www.fas.org.

Vladimir Putin, speech at the Russian embassy in Washington, DC, November 13, 2001, as quoted by Federal News Service, Inc. Reprinted by the Embassy of the Russian Federation, www.Russianembassy.org.

☆ Index ☆

★ Picture Credits ★

★ About the Author ★

Britta Bjornlund's keen interest in the relationship between the Soviet Union and the United States originated in high school when she began learning Russian and traveled to the Soviet Union for the first time. Currently a program manager at the Center for Russian Leadership Development at the Library of Congress, she holds a master's degree in international relations from the Johns Hopkins University School of Advanced International Studies (SAIS) and a bachelor's degree from Williams College.

Ms. Bjornlund has worked as an advisor to various government agencies throughout the former Soviet Union, and she witnessed the fall of the USSR firsthand in 1991. She lives in Washington, D.C., with her cat Trotsky and is an avid fan of the Washington Capitals ice hockey team.